中国精粹

HIGHLIGHTS OF CHINA

饮食养生卷
CHINESE DIET
AND HEALTH

孙维新 朱 旭 ◇编著
刘 川 王 菲 ◇译

全国百佳图书出版单位
时代出版传媒股份有限公司
安徽人民出版社

图书在版编目(CIP)数据

中国精粹·饮食养生卷/孙维新,朱旭编著;刘川,王菲译.—合肥:
安徽人民出版社,2015.9
ISBN 978－7－212－07711－2

Ⅰ.①中… Ⅱ.①孙…②朱…③刘… Ⅲ.①中华文化-通俗读物-汉、英
②食物养生-中国-通俗读物-汉、英 Ⅳ.①K203-49②R247.1-49

中国版本图书馆 CIP 数据核字(2015)第 143585 号

中国精粹·饮食养生卷
Zhongguo Jingcui · Yinshi Yangsheng Juan

孙维新　朱　旭　编著
刘　川　王　菲　译

出 版 人:胡正义	责任编辑:刘　超　陈　娟
责任印制:董　亮	装帧设计:陈　爽

出版发行:时代出版传媒股份有限公司 http://www.press-mart.com
　　　　　安徽人民出版社 http://www.ahpeople.com
　　　　　合肥市政务文化新区翡翠路 1118 号出版传媒广场八楼
　　　　　邮编:230071
　　　　　营销部电话:0551-63533258　0551-63533292(传真)
制　　版:合肥中旭制版有限责任公司
印　　制:安徽联众印刷有限公司

开本:700mm×1000mm　1/16　印张:7.25　字数:90 千
版次:2015 年 9 月第 1 版　2015 年 9 月第 1 次印刷

标准书号:ISBN 978－7－212－07711－2　　　定价:30.00 元

版权所有,侵权必究

目录

上篇 不厌其烦 不惮其精
——极端繁荣的饮食文化
一、四大菜系 / 13
二、茶文化 / 19
三、酒文化 / 24

下篇 "外练筋骨皮，内练一口气"
——展示生命力的中国武术
一、中国武术的精髓 / 33
二、中国武术的文化精神 / 46
三、中国武术的气功修炼 / 48

TABLE OF CONTENTS

PART 1 Splendid Chinese Cuisine

—— Thriving Chinese Cuisine Culture

1. Four Major Groups of Chinese Cuisine / 69

2. Tea Culture / 77

3. Wine Culture / 84

PART 2 Exercises of Bones, Muscles, Vitality and Breath

—— Chinese Martial Arts Designed to Improve Vitality

1. Marrow of Chinese Martial Arts / 94

2. Chinese Martial Arts, an Aspect of Chinese Culture / 106

3. Breathing Exercise of Chinese Martial Arts / 109

上篇

不厌其烦 不惮其精
——极端繁荣的饮食文化

"饮食男女，人之所欲也。"在中国，祖先圣贤形成了在性问题上保守的传统，而把人生的倾泻导向饮食。这个原因，不仅促进了烹调艺术的高度发展，而且赋予烹调以丰富的社会意义。首先，在人们的风俗习惯中，婚丧嫁娶这类大事，总是以吃饭为其重要内容甚至是高潮部分；其次，它是中国最重要的社交手段。在农村，"认识"这个词常常为"在一个桌上吃过饭"所代替。同时，烹调也是民族表达感情的重要方式。有朋自远方来，那友谊的分量一多半就要表现在洗尘的宴席上。在古代，甚至最郑重的国家领导工作也用"调和鼎鼐"这个典型的烹调名词来代表，足可在相当程度上反映出烹调的地位。

中国人善吃，也能吃。无论是地上跑的、天上飞的、水里游的，中国人无不拿来食用。西方人不吃动物内脏，而中国人却以为"吃啥补啥"，肝可以补血，肾可以补肾。"燕窝"是金丝燕在海边岩石间筑巢，吞下海藻后吐出的胶状物凝结而成的，古人认为可以补气，是一种珍贵的食品。熊掌、豹胎、凤髓、龙肝、马鞭、象鼻、鱼翅、猩唇都是美味。周王还备有特殊小菜"范"和"蜩"，即蜂蛹和蝉，广东民间的"烤桂花蝉"和"烤龙虱"（水甲虫），常一起出售，周人还吃醋老鼠……总之爱好极为广泛。不仅自然之物尽可以取用，中国人还善于创造。中国的素菜馆里常有"素腰花""素肠""素鱼"等菜，大多为豆制品，却可以乱真。尤其是中国的豆腐，无论贫贱老幼，无不爱食。制酱业也是中国的一项特殊成就，它以黄豆（或蚕豆）为主料，加适量的麦麸、淀粉、盐、糖等配料，利用毛霉菌的作用发酵而成。酱类不仅是一种优越的调味品，能增强食欲，而且含有多种发酵制成的酶，能促进人体复杂的化学变化，它的出现，对营养和保健，都是一大贡献。

就中西方饮食文化的比较来看：西方倾向于科学和营养，而中国则更倾向于艺术。饮食这件大事，在中国人看来不仅是填饱肚子的需要，更是一个艺术创造的过程。无论是烹调的准备，还是餐具的摆放、上菜的顺序、就餐的环境、食物的好坏、食客的数量……无不在考虑的范围之内。西方人烹制食物大多是一种纯粹的机械的工作，而中国则不然。街上卖烧饼的师傅，揉面时喜欢用擀面棒有节奏地敲打案板；庖丁解牛，"合于桑林之舞，乃中经首之会"；厨师在炒菜时，敲打铁勺，注意烹调的节奏感。这些自然不会对工作产生什么便利，但它却增加了艺术的要求。餐具的设计摆放也不是一件简单的事。富贵人家常有几十套餐具，什么菜配什么餐具，这都要用艺术家的眼光去衡量。唐、宋以来，中国的茶楼饭馆，大都选择在湖边或河边，采取园林式建筑，餐厅坐落于水榭花坛，竹径回廊之间，来客进入餐厅，如沐春风。清新的空气，幽雅的气氛，使人食欲大开。这种饭馆的设计，既合乎科学，又富有艺术感。就连菜的名称，也都洋溢着一种艺术的光辉。如黑鱼二吃，鱼骨烧汤，面上漂着一行豌豆，取名叫"一行白鹭上青天"，像诗一样美。其他如"翡翠上汤鸡""玉簪田鸡腿""百花酿鸭掌""大烩龙虎凤"等,都是文学与味蕾的完美结合。

中国饮食的要求颇为严格,它要求"色、香、味"俱全。所谓"色",既指菜肴的颜色,也指饮食的造型。中国的厨师们在颜色的搭配上、材料的雕刻设计上常能达到艺术家的水

菜肴的"色"与造型

准。唐懿宗咸通年间，同昌公主出嫁，皇上给公主送去一道菜，名叫"红虬脯"。它是用一尺长的红肉丝加工而成的佳肴，丝丝红肉，如一条条刚健有力的虬龙，给人以传神的动感，故称红虬脯。另据《南楚新闻》记载，南方的百越地区，有两种青蛙做成的菜肴，构思绝妙，其自然天成的艺术造型，不留丝毫人工雕镂的痕迹，令人叹为观止。中国菜家族中还有独特的一种——"看菜"。"看菜"既可观赏，又可食用，但以观赏为主。它的造型不仅精美绝伦，而且常带有一定的寓意，如"鱼"象征着"年年有余"等。拼字盛行于清代，清宫家宴和孔丘后裔向那拉氏进劝酒席，就习惯在盘菜中拼一些吉祥的词，如"洪福齐天""万寿无疆"之类，这是对形式的过分强调。

"香"指的是菜端上桌未食之前，就已异香扑鼻，让人食欲大开。中国人早就知道用调料炸出香味，制出浓香型的菜式，如酥香、油香、薰香、奶香、辛香、霉香、焦香、辣香、麻香、椰香、麻辣香、葱蒜香等。中国的厨房里大多油烟缭绕，难以清洁，但菜肴的气味却常可以香飘数家。这弥漫的香味吸引着羁旅漂泊的异乡人，也吸引着匆匆归家的行路人，并由此形成一种独特的情结，长期积淀在心里。归隐的诗人们坦率地歌咏着家乡的"鲈脍莼羹"，这记忆里的"香"总使人魂牵梦绕，不能忘怀！

各种调料

"味"指的是食品的品味。中国人吃饭,不仅吃营养,更重要的是"吃味"。对于某些非家常的烹调来说,食物甚至只是味道的载体。人们享用的是味道,即欣赏的是一种抽象的感觉。正因如此,西方人因鸡脚食之无肉,故将其与鸡骨、鸡毛视为同列而弃之,而在中国,鸡脚却是鸡身上较为贵重的部分。李笠翁自称为"蟹奴",就是因为蟹需细细品尝。过去有个笑话,讲的是上海人乘火车赶往外地,一天一夜的行程刚够吃完一只蟹。这种态度就缘于对"味"的极端重视。俗话说:"少吃多滋味",食物的品尝在中国是一件非常郑重的事。精细者常能发现最微小的差别,这样的人还被冠为"美食家"。中国人如被称为"好色",则大多带有贬义,但得到"美食家"这样的桂冠,却往往使人自豪而洋洋得意!

因为有了艺术的要求,所以对饮食的态度绝对是"食不厌精、脍不厌细"。中国人虽然在别的地方愿意偷懒,但却在饮食上从不嫌麻烦,他们不仅发明了多种的烹调方法,而且一道菜经过十道、几十道的工序是常有的事。举最常见的脍为例,脍是细切的鱼、肉,就是把肉切开,让肉分散,把瘦肉和肥肉分开,按不同的方法加工,然后把切好的肉放在一起。脍精细到极点,好的厨师能将肉切得像丝绸一样薄,像丝线一样细,出一口气,能将肉丝吹起来。这需要怎样的耐心和细心!《红楼梦》中刘姥姥吃的茄子,据说就要用净肉切成碎钉子,用鸡油炸了,再用鸡脯子肉和香菌、新笋、蘑菇、五香腐干、各色干果子一起切成钉子,用鸡油煨干,将香油一收,外加糟油一拌，盛在瓷罐里封严，要吃时还要用炒好的鸡爪来拌才行。工序之复杂令人难以想象！

就烹调方法而言，古人早就知道有焖、煮、烧、烤、烙、炙、烫、炸、蒸、脯、腌等多种方法。《齐民要术》介绍了多种烹调技艺，列举了近百款菜肴的名称及其做法，其中"炙法"就有20款。有的是装在竹筒里炙，有的是涂上泥炭，有的则是连烧带炙、连烹带炙。如张易之炙鸭鹅"为大铁笼，置鹅鸭于其内，当中热炭火，铜盆贮五味汁，鹅鸭烧火走，渴即饮汁，火炙痛旋转，表里皆熟，毛落尽，肉赤烘烘乃死"。虽然近乎残酷，但因为取其鲜活，仍为不少美食家喜爱。另外一款炙菜也别

烹调方法 炸

烹调方法 蒸

烹调方法 拔丝

烹调方法 炒

开生面,即竹筒烤杂肉,称"筒炙",做法是用鹅、鸭、獐、鹿、猪、羊肉细切捣软,调好味,加鸡蛋面粉拌匀,塞入竹筒,放在炭火上烧烤,烤熟,剖开竹筒即可食用。这种炙法的优点是不易烤糊,且带有竹的清香。

　　因为对食物的偏好,所以对于食物本身也颇有研究。中国医学将食物分成凉性、温性、热性和平性四种。热性、温性的食物均属阳性,多有祛寒、助阳生热、温中通络的作用。平性介于热性与凉性之间。凉性的食物属阴性食物，多有清凉泻火、解毒养阴的作用。掌握食物的属性，有助于医疗、保健。如冬天吃羊肉、狗肉，因其热性，有助于御寒；而夏天吃西瓜、绿豆汤，因其凉性，所以清热解火。

此外，不同的时令，适于不同的调味。"春多酸，夏多苦，秋多辛，冬多咸。"(《礼记·内则》)春天万物萌发，各种细菌容易污染食物，且乍暖乍寒，瓜菜青黄不接，胃口容易阻滞，这时应多调点酸，既杀菌，又开胃。夏天肉食吃多了易引起酸性反应，且水分消耗多，容易口干舌燥，如吃一顿苦瓜或饮一碗芥菜汤，就像服了一剂清凉饮料一样，顿时口齿清爽，胃肠舒适。秋天凉风熠熠，应该吃点热量略高而带刺激性的甘辛食品。冬天寒冷，需补充高热量的肉类食物，食盐的摄取量也随着增多，盐和胃酸结合，变成盐酸，能帮助对肉类的消化。这个按时令的调味的总结，是包含着一定的生理物理和生理化学知识的科学总结。

食疗学是中国医学和烹调学结合开出来的一朵瑰丽的奇花。中国第一部医典《内经》就指出："毒药攻养，五谷为养，五果为助，五畜为益，五配为埤(配)，气味合而服之，以养精益气。"也就是对付疾病，要使药物与营养相结合，即古人常说的"三分治疗七分养"。中国用来食疗的药膳有两种：一种是纯食物，可给没有病的人强身、健体、美容，如"味甘平，调中益气，可多食，令人好颜色"的樱桃、"去口臭，下气通神，轻身长年"的橘柚、"补中益气，强志除烦，久服轻身长年,不饥神仙"的大枣、"味甘平寒无毒,令人光泽、好颜色"的瓜子、"消渴利水道,益气力"的竹笋、"止漏血,出汗逐风湿"的生姜等;另一种则加入药物,可给有病的人治病。常见的有人参汤、阿胶汤、橘皮汤、茯苓膏、牡丹皮、地黄汤等,种类极多,功效也不错。中国古人留下的偏方中,大部分就是这种药膳。

  总之,中国的饮食文化极为繁荣。中国人对饮食的偏爱,不仅表现在饮食的质量上,而且表现在食物的数量上。中国人请客,主人在招待客人时常自谦说"菜烧得不好吃",却不会说"菜不够吃"。这是因为,中国的餐桌上的确非常丰富,必远远超过胃的负荷量,"撑死了"是不少人餐后抱怨的内容。南宋张俊宴请宋高宗的菜肴有102款,另有点心、水果、干果、雕花蜜饯、香药、咸酸等120碟。筵宴从早到晚,分成六个回合进行,中间穿插小菜、点心和水果、咸酸等。这么多的东西,就是找来十个彪形大汉作陪,个个具有特大的橡皮肚子,也难以全部咽下。清代所谓的"满汉全席",其实就是南北名菜名点的"组合大餐"。共计名菜100款,点心四五十种,另加干、鲜果品和开胃醒酒的酸酱泡菜之类一二十种。这种筵席一般要分三次进行,称"三撤席",要吃一整天。不仅富人家在吃上面穷尽奢侈,就连穷人偶尔请请客,也必让客人们吃得个肚大腰圆!中国人请客的这种态度,固然和其爱面子、讲排场有关,但归根结底归于他们对饮食的态度。饮食乃人生头等大事,中国的主妇们无论贵贱,都乐于做一两样拿手菜，因为在她们看来，牵住了男人的胃，即牵住了男人的心！

一 四大菜系

中国目前形成了四个大的地方菜系（当然细分不止此数），即苏系、粤系、川系和鲁系。现大略地介绍一下各大菜

肠粉

蒸凤爪

系的特色。

（一）粤菜

粤菜的发祥地是广州，它的头一个特点是用料广、选料严。而以海鲜及野味为上馔。如禽类，除了普通的三鸟，还常以鸽子、鹧鸪、鹌鹑、禾花雀等入馔。海鲜最推崇石斑、鲳鱼、鲜带子、明虾、膏蟹、海龟、鳗鱼等；野味最欣赏娃娃鱼、山瑞、甲鱼、山斑鱼、穿山甲、果子狸、龟、蛇等。粤菜选料很讲究，如做白切鸡，以清远鸡和文昌鸡为上乘；石斑鱼以老鼠斑为上乘；鲳鱼以白鲳为上乘；虾以近海明虾和基围虾为上乘；龟以金钱龟为上乘；鹅以黑鬃鹅为上乘。

米糕

三黄鸡

第二个特点是口味偏重清、鲜、爽、滑。做法以蒸、炒、溜居多。这与气候有一定关系，岭南炎热时间长，口感需要清爽；也是他们长期惯食海鲜和其他鲜活料，锻炼出追求原味的传统嗜好。岭南人对浓香型及油气重的菜，如开煲狗肉、炖扣肉、炸生蚝、红焖白鳝（海鳗）、红炖猪肘等，多在冬令来吃。

第三个特点是配菜丰富。这和物产丰富有关，粤北盛产冬菇，珠江三角洲一年四季都出产鲜草菇，还有竹笋、白木耳、石耳、石花菜等。由于气候适宜，四季时鲜不断，不论寒暑，都有嫩绿甘脆的蔬菜做佐料，还按时令以水果、香花入菜，如菠萝、荔枝、梅子、椰子、香蕉、凤梨、剑花、夜香花等，都是粤系做菜或做羹的良好佐料。粤菜佐料丰足，肉、蔬调配适宜，不腻喉，也符合饮食卫生。

第四个特点是粥品、点心特别丰富。由于岭南炎热的时间长，流汗消耗大，需要及时补充水分及易被吸收的养料，各类肉粥是较理想又较方便的食品。粥店（不少大饭店都兼有粥品）以老母鸡、猪骨、干贝、腐竹等熬好一大锅底粥，称为味粥，然后随时把味粥舀进小锅里，用鱼、虾、蟹、田鸡、肉丸、虾丸、猪杂、牛肉、鸡、鸭等预先备好的粥料，配以姜、葱、胡椒粉等，生滚出多种粥品，随时供应顾客。粤人善仿善创，广州又是长期中外交通的要道，粤式点心也特点丰富，吸取了中外许多点心的做法，各大茶楼饭店都有数百款点心的底单，使人百食不厌。

（二）川菜

川菜的发祥地是巴（今重庆）、蜀（今成都），它的一个很突出的特色是重油重味，偏爱麻辣，这与四川盆地的气候有关，雾多、阴天多、湿气重，麻辣使体表容易发散。四川人爱吃"毛肚"（以牛肚、牛杂为主料的重味麻辣火锅）、"麻婆豆腐"（这个菜具有麻、辣、油、烫、咸、嫩、滑七个特点）和其他一些麻辣菜式，都具有川菜的传统色彩。

另一个特点是善于运用普通材料，制成多种美味菜肴。如拿起一块半肥瘦猪肉，在四川厨师手里，可以做出美味的盐

麻婆豆腐

红油白肉

煎肉、回锅肉、荑（鱼）香肉（用泡菜、泡辣椒等为配料做成的香辣菜）、酱爆肉丁、锅巴肉片、甜烧白（豆沙、薯片夹扣肉）、咸烧白（香芋、芽菜夹扣肉）、粉蒸肉、咕噜肉、白煮麻辣肉等，每个菜都具有自己的个性。

四川人还善于做小吃，如麻辣牛头肉、怪味鸡、漳茶鸭子、酱兔肉、泡菜、汤圆、八宝糯米饭等，这是第三个特色。

（三）鲁菜

鲁菜，更确切的含义是齐、鲁菜，它的发祥地是临淄和曲阜，即齐、鲁的故都。它带有宫廷菜的余韵，它的头一个特点是用料讲究，善于以燕窝、鱼翅、鲍鱼、鱼肚、海参、鹿肉、蘑菇、银耳、蛤干玛油等高档材料，做出厚味大菜。

由于华北地区寒冷的时间较长，蔬菜品种又较少，练就了鲁菜厨师善于做高热量、高蛋白菜肴的本领，这是鲁菜的第二个特点。如脆皮烤鸭、九转肥肠（烧炸出来的猪大肠，可与烤鸭比美）、脱骨烧鸡（酥香离骨的烧鸡）、锅烧黄河鲤鱼、红烧海螺、炸蛎黄等，都是这类菜的佼佼者。

善于以汤调味，是鲁菜的第三个特点。鲁系厨师的传统习惯是在炒锅旁边备好一锅味汤（以老母鸡、猪蹄等为汤料），无论炒、溜、烧、扒，都以味汤溅锅，以代替味精，这是一个好传统。也善于做奶汤，济南的奶汤蒲菜，就久负盛名。

（四）苏菜

苏菜的发祥地是苏州和稍后的扬州和杭州。由于六朝和南宋的都城都在苏菜的地域，加上南北大运河通航一千多年，华东各大城镇成了南北人民长期交会的地点，为适应南北人的口味，苏菜的第一特点是味兼南北。苏系厨师既能做出清炒、清溜的南方爽口菜，又能做出像火腿炖肘子、狮子头、炒膳糊等高热量、高蛋白的美馔。苏菜的菜目中，让南北人都能接受的中心菜肴也特别多。

因为盛产湖蟹海鲜，所以河鲜菜特别突出，这是苏菜的第二个特点。如蟹黄狮子头、蟹黄燕窝、虾羹鱼翅、西湖糖醋鱼、清蒸鲫鱼（富春江特产）、鲜藕肉夹、浓汁太湖鲫鱼汤、莲子鸭羹等，都是苏系的著名河鲜菜。

扬州炒饭

盐水鸭

狮子头

苏式点心和小吃也很精美，这是第三个特点。如松子水晶肉甜糕、灌汤包子、蟹黄烧卖、宁波汤圆等，都是驰名全国的。

二 茶文化

茶，是中国人民的传统饮料。世界上，中国是种茶、制茶、饮茶最早的国家。古人讲"早晨起来七件事，柴米油盐酱醋茶"，可见茶在国人心中是非常重要的。

神农是中国远古时期的种植之神，传说茶就是他发现的。（"神农尝百草日遇七十二毒，得茶而解。"）最初的茶仅作为解毒的良药，以后经长期医疗实践，发现它不仅能治病，而且可以解热提神、清心明智，于是人们开始把它当作一种喜欢

茶圣陆羽像

的饮料。大量种植、采制，一时竟为时尚。而这时尚整整流行了两千多年。从时间传承上看，中国人饮茶的时间，几乎等同于埃及人建筑金字塔的时间。茶历经如此漫长的时间，尤其是在封建文化最为灿烂的时候，茶作为一种必不可少的宠物，参与了整个封建文化从无到有，从简单到辉煌，从兴到衰的整个过程，可以说它最能了解也最能代表中国古文化的精神追求。茶，在中国已成为一种文化的象征。

茶生于灵山妙峰，承甘露之芳泽，蕴天地之精华，而秉清灵、幽玄之禀性。它具有灵性而品格高贵，因此在古人那里它常被赋予"人格"的意义。对喝茶的讲究也就多了起来。首先，喝茶讲究环境。在室门内，则需凉台静屋、明窗净几；在旷野外，则需风和丽日、朗月清风。总之以僻静、清洁为好。明人最讲风雅，因此对此也最为注意。文震亨《长物志》言："构一斗室，相傍山斋，内设茶具，教一童专主茶役，以供长日清谈，寒宵兀坐。"并以为这是"幽人"的首要大事，不可或缺。富人在室中专设饮茶的茶寮，而闲人雅士则更爱在山中林下品饮。"何处茶烟起，渔舟系竹西"、"寂寞南山下，茶烟出树林"，幽雅、淡泊之意自生。

饮茶离不开水，古往今来的饮茶大师们无不讲究对水的选择。没有好水，再好的茶叶也泡不出好的味道。陆羽是世界上第一部饮茶专著《茶经》的作者。他在书上专门有一章节论述取水的学问，他认为泡茶最好的水是山中之水，其次是江中水，最次是井水。而且山中之水也要选择"乳泉、石池漫流者"，汹涌直泻的不能要。宋代以降，品水越精，不少学者也专有论述。到清时，乾隆每至一处，必命侍从汲其泉水，然后称其轻重，依次排出新的等级，定北京玉泉为第一，其次是塞上伊逊泉、济南珍珠泉、杨子金山泉……其排列的标准无非是水的活、轻与甘洌。古人也有用雨水、冰水、露水、雪水等来煎茶的。一是取其鲜活，利于养生；二是求其雅趣。《红楼梦》中的妙玉即是品水专家，她取梅花上的雪，埋在地下五年才饮。这哪是平凡人所能饮得的，非得仙人才配！

烹茶用的火也不能随便。古人认为一般柴火煎出来的茶会带有木的异味，且其火势浮，煎水不力。因此要用木炭来煎，而且最好是用硬柴烧成的炭。如果是非硬柴烧的炭，或炭没烧尽，都会有柴烟，一旦串入汤内，会改变汤的质地。古人称这种火烟为"茶魔"，而将好的炭火称为"汤友"。古人又把好炭火称为"活火"，一方面是无烟，另一方面则有较猛的火焰。因而在煎水前，先要将炭中的余烟烧尽，取其性力炽猛的部分，放上火器，再很快地扇动炉中之火，愈快愈好，不要停手，使炭火始终保持向上腾活的状态。苏轼便曾数次提到这种活火的功夫。《试院煎茶》中云："君不见，昔时李生好客手自煎，贵从活火发清泉"，《汲江煎茶》："活水还须活火煎。"

观汤。唐宋以来，这道程序颇为精细。唐人煮水用的"釜"（其功能类似于宋代的铫、瓶），上端敞口，可用以观察水的沸滚程度，其观汤方式则曰"形辨"。过熟的汤泡出的

茶圣陆羽像

茶没有香味，古人对此十分计较。陆羽按滚沸的状态把汤分为三种："其沸如鱼目，微有声，为一沸；缘边如涌泉连珠，为二沸；腾波鼓浪，为三沸。"何时冲泡为好，各人看法不一。宋人有"背二涉三"说，即在听到水已二沸时，取出最好。明人许次纾则认为"水一入铫，便须急煮。候有松声，即去盖，以消息其老嫩。蟹眼之后，水有微涛，是为当时。"虽是一家之言，但也不无道理。

  品茶艺术所追求的整体效果，还反映在其饮用杯具的讲究上。冯正卿在《岕茶笺》中写道，饮茶要以壶小为贵。每人持一壶，任其自斟自饮。壶小的作用，是使茶的香味不易散荡。因为茶的香味在冲泡之后不先不后，只有一时呈现。喝得太早则香味还未充分体现，喝得太迟则香味却易散荡。只有在恰到好处的时候饮用，才能得到茶香的妙趣。因此，他主张人各持一壶，反对分散斟倒，认为只有这样品茶者才能在茶香呈现恰到好处时一饮而尽。除此以外，对茶器的造型、色泽，以及质地，都有较高的要求。陆羽偏爱越州的瓷器，认为越州青瓷能将杯具和茶汤融为一体，有一种和谐美。而宋人蔡襄则以为"茶色白，宜黑盏"，讲究的是对比美。审美趣味的不同，导致各自偏爱的不一样，但无不都以越精美越好。据传明代最好的杯具，"值十万钱"，可见世人对茶具的重视程度。

  茶可独饮，也可与朋友、来客共享。独处的时候，心情必愉悦、闲适、舒坦、清静，欣欣然自有"尘心洗静心难尽"的兴奋，这样才配饮茶。而与朋友共处的时候，唯神气相通者才能与之共饮。许次纾《茶疏》"论客"一节中对何种情境下适于茶饮作了明确规定：凡是"宾朋杂沓"，以酒相待；遇到"乍会泛交"，只需一般家备的果品招待即可；只有逢上"素心同调"，双方都很"畅适"，能"清言友辩，脱略形骸"者，才可呼童篝火，酌水点汤。备茶的简繁程序，则视客多少而定，如果三人以下，就只烹一炉；如五六人，便需要两鼎；如果客人太多，就只得暂时停火，不以茶来招待了。可见，虽是共饮，仍讲究心气精神的"幽"和"静"。

总之，中国人对茶的态度，确实是其他民族所没有的。它讲究品味与情调的高雅，环境与氛围的幽静，水质的性灵与清纯，杯具的洁净与名贵，对象、知己的亲切与神会，这都不是能一言以蔽之的。中国艺术的风格是含蓄。中国人的品茶，虽在汤色的鉴别与欣赏的过程中得到愉悦和快乐，其真正的目的却是通过对茶味的探辨，到达悟与获的境界。而茶中之味就不仅仅是茶之味，而是人生之味，对宇宙体味之味了。

三 酒文化

中国是世界上酿酒最早的国家之一。《战国策·魏策二》说酒的创始人是夏禹时代的仪狄；《说文》除了说仪狄之外，还说是周人杜康。因此古人又常把"杜康"称为酒的代名词。曹操诗云："何以解忧？唯有杜康。"

酒在中国也被认同为一种特殊的文化活动，深深镶嵌在中国人的心中。穷人可以喝它,"日日有酒当汤饮","无酒待客主人愧","家家扶得醉人归";富人也可以喝它,喝到"酒池肉林""朱门酒肉臭"的地步。从壮士出征到庆功祝捷,从婚寿喜宴到缔结盟约,一系列重大的活动无不有它。清明扫墓,坟前供之以酒,坟头洒之以酒。远古时期古人占卜问卦,农耕时代古人求雨祭典,民俗活动时的迎神送鬼,叩拜神灵,无不施之以酒,仿佛无酒不成敬意。酒便是这样以茶所不能替代的身份,贯穿在这一系列庄严神圣的场合,甚至对于对待即将开刀问斩的囚犯,都有祭酒以显送他上天的宽宏大量。中国民众对于酒的特殊情感和集体认同,就可见一斑了。

酒的种类很多。按所酿之时来分类,可分为春酒、百日

绍兴黄酒

酒、一宿酒等。按所用原料分,则有米酒、麦酒、椒酒、葡萄酒、菊花酒、梅花酒、桂花酒、榆酒、马乳酒等。米酒、麦酒的原料是稻米、麦、稷、高粱等。椒酒是用椒实泡制的酒。葡萄酒是鲜葡萄或干葡萄酿成,此酒从西域传来。菊花酒是采菊花及其茎、叶与黍米混合酿成。梅花酒、桂花酒的酿制基本与菊花酒相似。榆酒用榆荚酿成。马乳酒由马奶酿成。不同地域的人对酒的偏爱也不一样。南方主要喝黄酒。黄酒是中华民族独有的世界上最古老的酒种之一,始于夏商时期,又称老酒。中国的黄酒,以浙江绍兴黄酒最为有名。而在北方则是白酒的天下,白酒是中国的传统曲种,按发酵类型分固态发酵白酒、液态发酵白酒和半固态发酵白酒,按用曲分有大曲白酒、小曲白酒和麸曲白酒,按香型分有清香型白酒、浓香型白酒、酱香型白酒、米香型白酒和其他香型白酒。高粱酒是北方人的最爱,它已成为北方壮士豪情壮志与激情满怀的象征。

中国酒家族中,药酒的历史也十分悠久。酒本身即能治病,据《胜饮篇·功效》引王莽诏令:"酒为百药之长,盖酒本黄帝用以治疾也。"酒有发散促进血液循环的功能,可以去风湿,因而西汉袁盎作吴王刘濞相国时,他侄儿劝他"宜日饮酒"。华佗做手术时用的麻醉药麻沸散,也是和酒而服,以减轻患者的痛苦。中国人更在酒中加药,以养身滋补、强体壮身。如蛇酒,用以祛风去湿;人参酒,用以延缓衰老;三鞭酒,用以固本壮阳;虎骨酒,用以治疗跌打损伤、健骨强身等。中国的医学名著《本草纲目》,就列数了几十种药酒配方,把名贵中药材加到酒中去治病,这在世界酒林中独树一帜。

汉代已有专门卖酒的街市。《汉书·游侠传》记载:"酒市赵君都、贾子光,皆长安名豪报仇怨以刺客者也。"说明长安城内已有酒市。南北朝时的《洛阳伽蓝记·法云寺》记载得更加清楚:"市西有延酤、治觞二里,里内之人多酿酒为业。"酒家为了招来客人,广开生意,常常在门前高悬酒帘。《韩非子》曰:"宋人有沽酒者,悬帜甚高。"这是最早的宣传广告。垆,是放酒坛的台。古人常把"美酒"与"佳人"联系起来,因此多有"美人当垆(站柜台)"的传说,如"文君当垆""胡姬当垆"等。

酒有双重属性。一方面它扮演着跃马横刀、威风凛凛、豪气万丈的角色。"葡萄美酒夜光杯,欲饮琵琶马上催。"酒神催人进取、使人豪放。另一方面,酒神又使人悲观,使人颓废。"借酒浇愁愁更愁",它给清醒的愤世者以昏沉与安睡。更有甚者,为酗酒而出事,为酒醉而丧生。古人说人生四害:酒、色、财、气,酒高居其首。嗜酒与好色结合在一起,称为酒色之徒。

然而酒醉虽会使人丑态百出,东倒西歪,满口胡言,但中国人却偏爱在酒席上使人醉倒。西方人喝酒多为品酒,而中国人请客饮酒却非让人醉,这种颇有意思的现象,隐含着两层含意。

一、主人的慷慨大方。因为就一般情况而言,酒需要下酒菜，所以，并非人人都可以天天喝到酒。因此，他们认为愈能提供挥霍无度的滥饮，愈能表示主人的热情。中国人平素节俭，而宴席上的挥霍，也许是对平素节俭的一种放纵。

二、喝酒是要有限度。超过限度就要醉。注重礼仪的中国人平素过着宁静无争的生活。喝酒时，喧闹的划拳，各式各样的饮酒游戏，会时时引发发泄般的喧哗、斗杀般的呐喊，这仿佛也是他们对生活的另一种解释。

那么，怎样才能多喝酒呢？"敬酒不吃吃罚酒"，这句俗语讽刺的是那种不识好歹的人和事，然而，饮酒时的情形却不是这样了。中国人发明了花样繁多的罚酒游戏，目的就是为了使人喝酒。事实上，饮酒时假如没有罚酒的那种诱使的劝导和道德化了的罚酒约定，饮酒的热烈便难体现，而罚酒的这种约定却在强迫性质中浸透着热情与好客的真诚。我们应该看到这种独特的文化现象隐含着戏谑的潜质及游戏的快感。

罚酒的方法多种多样，有时显得斯文和智慧，如"行酒令"。酒令是饮酒时一种助兴行乐的游戏。具体方法是：推一人为令官，行令之权，不论饮者尊卑，一概听令，或轮流作诗词，或轮流做其他游戏，倘参与者因才疏学浅、不够机敏而败阵，就得罚酒。行酒令在达官贵人中很普遍，《红楼梦》里那些才思敏捷的小姐就常以行酒令取乐。

有时也显得粗犷而豪放，如民间的"划拳"。划拳系中国人的一独创，日本据说也有，但据考证乃是中国传入。划拳的口令因地随俗变化多端，也因时代习尚差异而更换内容。无论这些口令如何变化，终不离从一到十这十个数字，猜拳的双方，各自均以喊出的数字与拳指现出的数字相连。甲方亮出的数字与乙方亮出的数字相加一旦恰巧与乙方喊定的数字相符，那么甲方就必定要被罚酒了。于是，猛烈挥动着拳头，纷繁变化着手指，一方面还要不停地报出数字，并且还要时刻留心对方的手势变化与数字的闪现。一声高过一声的激唱，近乎于争斗或吵架，但并非恶意。赢家自然在喧嚣中得到了兴奋与满足，输家愈躲闪愈推却，却愈招来人们的讥笑与嘲弄，然而这却是一种不乏真诚的友好。喝酒也因此有了一种娱乐的快乐。

　　有时罚酒却又从属于天意。让偶然来决定人的输赢，这是中国人的宿命观，在饮酒上也有体现，如流行的游戏"曲池流觞"和"击鼓传花"。用水流推动浮杯，让其在曲槽中流动，因水流速的急缓不可知，杯滞留于什么地方也不可知。杯停在谁面前，谁就必须接受罚酒。同样，在鼓点声中传递花束，一旦鼓声停花也必须停下，而停止的花束落到谁手上，谁就要接受罚酒。因为结果皆是不可预料的事，因此当事人心中往往异常紧张，而又正是这造成了喝酒中的乐趣。

　　总之，茶和酒几乎代表了中国人的一切理想与追求。酒投合、激发人的世俗欲望，而茶则涤除、消停人的这一欲望；酒多与混沌、冲乱的心智相连，而茶则导人趋于清明、爽远；喝酒时奔放纵情的豪饮，很容易让人联想起士大夫

"达能兼济天下"的壮志，而饮茶时的收敛与宁静，则更趋向于文人雅士的"穷则独善其身"的无奈。面对着茶，人们自然而然会恭顺谦和、温文尔雅，而面对着酒，豪饮是热情，酒量是风度。

下篇

外练筋骨皮 内练一口气
——展示生命力的中国武术

武术又称国术或武艺,中国的传统体育项目。它把踢、打、摔、拿、跌、击、劈、刺等动作按照一定规律组成徒手和器械的各种攻打格斗功夫、套路和单势练习。

中国武术的起源可以追溯到原始社会。那时人们就已开始用棍棒等原始工具作武器同野兽进行斗争,后来为了互相争夺财富,进而制造了更具有杀伤力的武器。武术开始只是军旅武术,后逐渐流传于民间,成为民间武术。明代是中国武艺大发展的时期,出现了不同风格的技术流派,拳术、器械都得到了发展,特别是在理论上总结了过去的练武经验,具有代表性的著作有《纪浓薪书》《武篇》《耕余剩枝》等。这些著作不同程度地记载了拳术、器械的流派、沿革、动作名称、特征、运动方法和技术理论等,有的还附有歌诀及运动图解,为后世研究武术提供了重要依据。

今天的武术运动主要包括拳术、器械和对练三个方面。拳术有长拳、太极拳、南拳、形拳、八卦等;器械可分为兵器、短兵器、软兵器;对练包括徒手对练、器械对练。武术是中华民族创造和发展起来的体育活动,是宝贵的文化遗产之一。

中国武术的精髓

武术以其健美的姿势、高难的动作,给人以美和力的享受,通过不懈的锻炼可强身健体。武术的"武"有"打"之意,而"术"指方法和技术。所以,武术的精髓是以起、落、钻、翻、退、摇、转、踢、打、摔、拿等组合而成的实用价值极高的连环技击招法。

连环招法是御敌交手时，一招连一招，一招破一招，一招比一招紧，一招比一招快，击败对手的技击招法，因此，踢、打、摔、拿之中，手法、腿法、身法差之毫厘，不但制不住敌方，还会因一瞬间的毫厘之差而被对方打倒，所以中国武术讲究悟透瞬间和毫厘之差的秘密，应用自如地技击继而掌握武术的精华。

掌握武术真谛，中国武术强调一靠名师指点，二靠自己潜心研练，悟彻拳理，做到真正艺上身。练拳练到"拳无拳，艺无艺，无艺之中是真艺"的程度。

武当拳

武当拳

　　中国武术强调化境，即武功达到炉火纯青的境界，化境历来是有志练武者孜孜以求的目标。从技击角度来评判武术的水平可分成三个等级。一是下乘，没有掌握武技之"术"；二是中乘，应敌时能聚精会神，恪守章法，凭技巧与功力进行搏击以争取胜利；三是上乘，临敌时随意出手，应付自如，克敌制胜，达到化境的地步。

　　武术的化境是靠"熟练"达到的，是高度熟练的技巧和极其深厚的功力造成的。因此，许多练武之人穷其毕生精力练习武术，效法上乘，依靠自己刻苦研练和实践，从自然的本能走向必然的王国，达到出神入化的境地。

　　在中国武术中拳术是所有练武之人必须学习掌握的。中国拳种，目前有详尽历史源流、相对完整的理论、技术体系的拳种共计192种,如以山头划分的少林、武当派;以内外家划分拳种;以长江、黄河流域的地域划分等。而基本拳术有长拳、太极拳、南拳、形意拳、八卦掌、匣脊拳、翻子拳、地趟拳、劈拴拳、螳娜拳、八极拳、猴拳、醉拳、华拳、花拳、鹰爪拳、绵拳、六合拳、蛇拳、意拳、少年拳、查拳等。

其中,八卦掌原名"转掌",又称"游身八卦掌""八卦连环掌",是以掌法变换和行步走转为主的拳术。由于其运动方式纵横交错、形与《周易》八卦图方位暗合,故取名"八卦掌"。八卦掌使用技击法则,可以用"攻守兼备"四个字来概括。其讲究"动敌之将动,静敌之先静,敌刚我柔,敌老我逸,敌退我进,敌动我动,动中观敌,动中运便,敌来我攻,破攻并进,敌来我解,而后还击,敌不动我也动。"具体实战

八卦掌

时，强调不与敌方做正面的冲突，注重以外侧向中心进攻的战略战术。

八极拳，全称"开门八极拳"，又称"岳山八极拳"。称"开门"者，取其以六种开法（六大开）作为技法核心，破开对方门户（防守架子）之意。称"八极"者，系沿用古代有"九州之外有八寅，八寅之外有八宏，八宏之外有八极"的说法，寓"八方极远"之意。称"岳山"者，相传八极源自河南焦作岳山寺，故名冠"岳山"。

八卦掌

少林拳

　　八极拳以六大开、八大招为技术核心，套路有八极小架、八极拳（亦称"八极对接"）、六肘头、刚功八极、八极新架、八极双轨等。器械以陆合大枪、对扎大陆合为主。其劲道讲求崩、撼、突、击、挨、戳、挤、靠以及撞靠劲、缠捆劲等。特点为动作简洁、长短相兼、发劲迅猛、撞靠捆跌突出、肘法叠用、下盘稳固。新中国成立后，随着武术运动的发展，八极拳被列为全国性竞赛项目之一。

　　白眉拳是中国拳术中南拳之一。传说是四川峨眉山白眉道人所传，现有四川、广东、香港、澳门等地较流行。其特点是刚强凶猛，连贯性强，路线宽广，其拳法有鞭拳、双撞拳及千字箭拳，桥法有碎桥、钻桥、刹桥与封桥等。腿法有同影侧踢（即撑鸡脚）与蹬脚等。其主要拳套有小十字、大十字、三六八卦、十八摩桥功及猛虎出林等。

少林拳是长拳类代表拳种之一，广义的少林拳，指少林派，狭义的少林拳，指嵩山少林寺僧众传习的拳术。少林拳还包括少林寺中传习的兵械。在清朝，少林寺公开的传习内容是易筋经、八段锦，以及一些传统的导引健身术。明末清初至清咸丰年间，少林拳术由外家拳参合内家，内外技法融溶，由原来重练外刚、主于搏人，向"内外交修"演进。少林拳发展到近现代，运动特点表现为拳禅一体、神行一片，硬打快攻，齐进步齐退。少林的套路一般都较短小，运动路线多呈直线往返。少林拳的动作姿势要求，头端面正；眼注一点，兼顾上下左右；头竖不偏，随身变转；开胸直腰，不能松塌；裹胯合膝，微扣脚尖，不能敞档开膝外摆脚尖；肩要下松，手臂击出要曲而不曲、直而不直，以便曲防时含有攻意，直攻时含有

少林拳

守意。身法注重控制重心,动则轻灵,静则沉稳。步架要求进步低,退步高,动作整体表现为全身上下内外协调一致。动作时,步催、身催、手催,以迅疾见功夫。少林拳套路很多,有小洪拳、大洪拳、老洪拳、罗汉拳、昭阳拳、梅花拳、炮拳、七星拳、柔拳等,对练套路有扳手六合、咬手六合、耳把六合、踢打六合等。此外,还有"心意把"等散招练习法。

查拳,亦称"叉拳""插拳"。因此拳多用"揸"法讲究出手即'揸',其枪诀中有"一揸二拿三扎花"。查拳的特点有三:(1)节奏鲜明,动迅静定;(2)动作紧凑,拳路清晰;(3)势整力顺,眼疾手快。要求做到"行如风,站如钉,起如猿,落如鹰",动如猛虎,静如山岳;快慢相间,刚柔相济,招法清楚,急转突停。无论攻守进退,快而不乱,慢而不散,姿势工整舒展。手眼身步均要上下相随,前后相连,内外相合,并有"三节"、"六合"、"十要"(即缩、小、绵、软、巧、错、速、硬、脆、滑十字攻防要诀)。其手法有冲、撩、劈、盖、挑、搂、插、砍等;身法有闪、转、折、翻、冲、撞、挤、靠等;腿法有蹬、弹、踢、蹦、踹、穿、点等;步法有进、退、绕、插、行、转等;眼法有定、注、随、凝等,要求眼到手到,目随势注,势换目移,"意欲往左先往右,势欲向前先向后"。套路中多有蹿蹦跳跃,起伏转折。查拳共有十路:一路母子,二路行手,三路飞脚,四路开平,五路关东,六路埋伏,七路梅花,八路连环,九路龙摆尾,十路串拳,一、二路各有副拳一套。器械有查刀、查枪、查钩、查剑等长短单双多种，基础训练辅有炮拳、滑拳、洪拳、腿拳及十路弹腿，另有多种对练套路。长拳规定套路中曾吸收部分查拳内容，亦收入全国体育院系通用武术教材。

太极拳，"太极"一词源出《周易》，是指天地未分之前，元气混而为一的状态。《周易》传为周文王的著作。其中《系辞上篇》说："是故，易有太极，是生两仪。两仪生四象；四象生八卦；卦定吉凶。" 过去的文理学家曾有解释："太极者，无称之称，不可得而名；取有之所极，况之太极者也"，"太极谓天地未分之前，元气混而为一，即是太初。太一也。" 由此可知，太极就是我们所知的宇宙的原初，是我们生活的世界的原始。不过这只是中国哲学的见解，不是科学的论断。太极拳的源流甚远，来自民间的多种拳术，经过历代人不断地完善和再编排才成为近百年流传的太极拳套路。

太极拳的特点是意识（心）、呼吸（息）、动作（身）三者紧密结合，运动时要示求心静神聚，舒松自然，"神为主帅，身为躯使"，"动之则分，静之则合"，"一动无有不动，静无有不静"，"动中求静"不尚拙力；气如车轮，腰如轴，如环无端，绵绵不断；呼吸根蒂，气沉丹田；专气至柔，纯任自然。外形"静如山岳，动若江河"，有圆、柔、慢、稳、匀几大特点。动作开展大方，协调性特别强。所有运动过程都是阴阳对立的统一体。 各式太极拳均有这些特点，因而太极拳理论是同一的，不因动作表现形式的不同，流派不同而异。太极拳的流派传比较有代表性的有五大流派，即陈、杨、吴、武、孙等五式太极拳。

陈式太极拳创始于明末清初的著名拳师陈王廷，据《温县志》记载在明思宗崇祯十四年（1641）任温县"乡兵守备"，明亡后隐居家乡，晚年造拳自练、教授弟子儿孙。

杨式太极拳，由河北永年人杨露禅从学于河南温县陈家沟陈长兴，与其子杨健侯、其孙杨澄甫等人在陈式老架太极拳的基础上，创编发展了"杨式太极拳"。其拳路逐渐删改了陈式老架中原有的纵跳、震足、发劲等动作，由杨健侯修订为中架子，又经杨澄甫一再修订逐渐定为杨式大架子，即现在广为流行的杨式太极拳。

武式太极拳，清末河北永年人武禹襄在杨露禅从陈家沟返乡后，深爱其术，从学杨于陈式老架太极拳，后又从陈清平学赵堡架，经过修改，创造了"武式太极拳"。

吴式太极拳，杨露禅在从陈家沟拳师陈长兴处学得太极拳，后传入北京，创立杨式太极拳。杨露禅在北京传习拳艺，在旗营从军的旗人全佑得其传授，后又拜其子杨班侯为师，成为太极拳一代宗师。最终创立吴式太极拳。

孙式太极拳，河北完县人孙禄堂，自幼酷爱武术，从师李魁垣学形意拳，继而学于李之师郭云深，又从师程廷华学八卦掌。经多年研练，功夫深厚。后双从师郝为真学太极拳，参合八卦、形意、太极三家拳术的精义，融合一体而创"孙式太极拳"。

在中国武术遗产中，峨眉派武术犹如"一树开五花，五花八叶扶，皎皎峨眉月，光辉满江湖"（清初湛然法师《峨眉拳铺》语）而与少林派、武当派并重。峨眉派武术的特点是兼备佛家与道家之长，既吸收了道家的动功，又有佛家禅修的基础，独创了一套动、静功相结合的练功方法。这种练功方法与各种拳术、器械套路及散打技艺结合一起，组成了峨眉派武术体系。峨眉派理论上主张动功与静功并重，在动功上有十二桩："天、地、之、心、龙、鹤、风、云、大、小、幽、冥"。静功上讲究六大专修功："虎步功，重捶功，缩地功，悬囊功，指穴功，涅槃功"，其中尤以"指穴功"的三十六式天指穴功最具威力，既可按摩治病，又可作为武功制敌。

  峨眉派武术善用五峰六肘之力。五峰即头、肩、肘、臀、膝；六肘指上肘、下肘、左肘、右肘、回肘、倒肘。攻防技术上讲究手脚灵活。"腾、挪、闪、颠、浮、沉、吞、吐"是峨眉派的主要技击方法。

  在中国武术中，武术的器械也是很重要部分。武术的器械有刀、剑、枪、棍、双刀、双剑、双枪、双勾、九节鞭、流星锤、绳标等。常见的和普及面较广的武术器械有刀、剑、枪、棍。武术中的刀术是以缠头裹脑和劈、砍、撩）挂等动作为主，并配合另一手的辅助动作和各种步型、跳跃组成套路。动作只有勇猛、雄健、有力等特色。剑术是以点、崩、刺、撩、劈、挂等动作和另一手所做的剑指，配合各种步型组成套路。它的动作轻快、飘洒，刚柔相济，舞姿优美。枪术是长兵器的一种，以拦、拿扎等动作为基础，配合舞花动作构成套路。它

短刀　　　　　　　尖刀

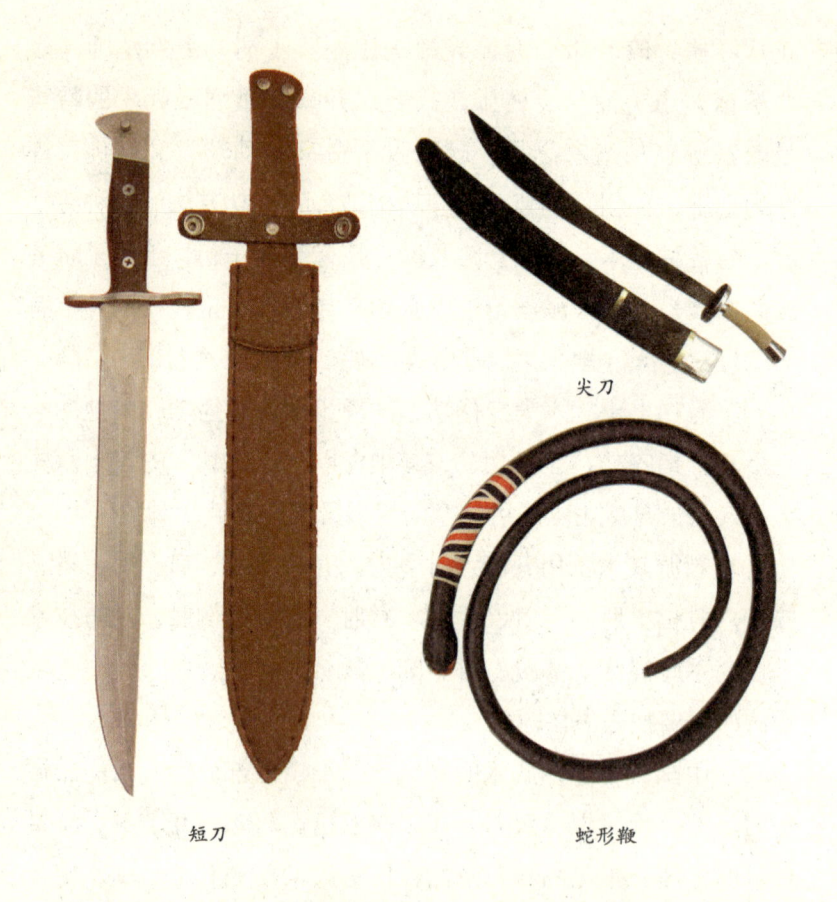

蛇形鞭

表现出刚柔相济、变化多端的特色。棍术主要是以抡、劈、戳、撩、云、舞花等动作构成套路。它的动作特点是勇猛快速、刚劲有力。

此外，在中国武术中还有"十八般武艺"之说。"十八般武艺"，泛指各种武艺，并非固指武艺的十八种内容。其内容有多种说法。其一，"若论着十八般武艺，弓弩枪牌、戈矛剑戟、鞭链挝锤。"（明代臧晋叔辑《元曲选·逞风流王焕百花亭》）其二，"那十八般武艺：矛锤弓弩铳、鞭简剑链挝、斧钺并戈戟、牌棒与枪扒。"（元明间施耐庵著《水浒全传·第二回》）其三，"十八般：一弓、二弩、三枪、四刀、五剑、六矛、七盾、八斧、九钺、十戟、十一鞭、十二锏、十三挝、十四殳、十五叉、十六把头、十七绵绳套索、十八白打。"（明万历间谢肇淛《五杂俎》），后来还出现了"九长九短"、"六短十二长"，以及"大十八般"、"小十八般"等武艺内容说。综合历代"十八般武艺"的内容，删去重复，共包括下述种目，属抛射兵械的有弓、弩、箭矢、铳；属长兵器的有戈、矛、枪、棍、杵、杆、杖、棒、斧、钺、戟、（长杆）大刀、把头、扒、挝、铲；属短兵器的有

月牙刀

剑、（短柄）刀、鞭、锏、钩、镰、锤、拐、环；属软兵器的有链、流星、绵绳、套绳；属徒手的武艺统称为"白打"。这些种目，基本反映了中国古代武艺的概貌。

二 中国武术的文化精神

中国武术作为中国文化的一个有机组成部分和独特表现形式，从一个侧面反映出整个中国文化的基本特征。

中国武术源远流长，它融会了中国的哲学、医学、兵法、技艺、教育、美学等，在一个特定的方面集中地表现了中华民族的性格和智慧。中国武术的特征，是"以心行气、以气运身""手眼身法步，精神气力功""刚柔并济、内外合一""形神兼备体用两全"的心理活动，敌我攻防格斗的思想意识，龙腾虎跃、纵横往来、起伏跌宕、圆转变化的节奏韵律，以智巧取、顺势借力、"牵动四两拨千斤"的机智技能。上虚下实中间灵，重视下盘功夫，往往先让一步，留有余地，有理、有利、有节，稳字领先，讲究稳、准、狠。

中国武术的历史形成，有它的学术渊源、技术演化和师承源流三个方面。它的拳理阐释，主要依托于中国古典哲学；它的应敌原则，主要依托于中国古典兵法；它的演练功法，主要依托于中国古典医学。中国武术的技术演化，则跟中国古代的文化技术形态，特别是其中的作战方式、艺术趣味和养生技术的演变联系在一起；分别经历了依托于力量和勇气的"武勇"，依托于技巧和智谋的"武艺"和相对规范化、程式化的"武术"这样三大阶段。

它的第一条演化路线，是把古代导引养生技术跟军事攻防格斗技术融合在一起；

它的第二条演化路线，是把一些攻防格斗动作加以典型化和艺术化，并把它跟舞蹈和杂技结合起来；

它的第三条演化路线，是把形体训练跟思想训练结合起来，提炼出一整套"身心合一"的"修性"技术。

中国武术首先所要解决的是人体内部的心、身关系，所谓"外练筋骨皮，内练一口气"。中国武术无论哪个流派，都强调"意到、气到、劲到"，通过一种自觉的、身心运动去平衡阴阳、调和气血、疏通经络、增强体质、培植力量。它通过"体、用"关系上升为技击领域，又把人体内部的心、身关系

动功 健身气功

对象化为人体外部的敌我关系，所谓"因敌应变、示形造势、虚实变换、奇正生克"，中国武术无论哪个流派，都强调"守中取势"和"得机得势"。这个层次的社会功能，主要是防身、御敌、制人、取胜。它还通过"舍己从人"达到"从心所欲"而实现复归，上升到哲学领域，是所谓"天人合一"，是有无、动静、阴阳、心物、主客的高度统一，是客观规律性和主体能动性相互融合的产物。这个层次的社会功能，主要是修心、养性、悟道、怡情。这时它破除了各种偏执，对世俗的各种胜负、成败、利害、得失，采取一种超脱的"游戏"态度。交手应敌，并不是心浮气躁地跟对手拼老命，而是心平气和地跟对手"认真"地"玩"上两手，这恰好就是人所特有的自由自主活动，是人摆脱各种依赖关系后的独立发展本身。因此说，中国武术不只是一种体育技术和技击技巧，它还是一种思维方式、人生态度和人格修养。中国武术无论行功走架还是交手应敌，都不但十分讲究招式劲力，而且还极其讲究性情志趣，有一种超越于技术本身的博大精深的武术精神。

三 中国武术的气功修炼

气功，是中国武术中一种强身健体、开发潜能的修炼方法。在广义上，它不仅仅指中国气功修炼方法，还包涵了气功的要旨，以开发人体潜能为目的相关理论、功法。现今气功可分为这样几种类型。

灵子类（自发功），相传是古代真正的巫者所修炼的功法，练这种功法的人相信在人体内部有一种被称为灵子的物质，它不但是组成人的灵魂的必要物质，而且也是潜意识的一种存在载体。修炼此种功法的要诀是让灵子来控制自己，通过潜意识发挥作用，从而做出一些自发性动作，达到使身体的潜在能量得到锻炼和加强的目的。此功主要用于给自己或他人治病、疗伤。代表性功法：灵子显动术。

内丹类，源于道家，是由古代的炼丹术演变而来的炼内丹功法。后来引入了《易经》的思想，使内丹术发生了巨大的飞跃。因此内丹术属于道家和儒家两大流派的杂合产物。练这种功法的人坚信练成后如同服食了金丹，可以长生不老，也因

太极拳

动功 健身气功

　　为这种信念，才使人们长期不断追求，以致这种功法成为主要流派，形成了一套复杂且完整的体系。这种功法以成就大道为目的，不刻意追求神通。

　　武术类，起源无从考证，通过修炼人体内的气，再用一定方式运用内气，临时性地激发出人体的一些潜能，从而取巧制敌。如轻功、硬气功等。

　　藏密类，是从西藏起源的气功，是完全属于开发人体潜能的。有一套十分完善的理论体系，通过不同的轮回修持，由最初的事业部，最终修完无上瑜伽部。修炼特征是：在于口持真言，手结契印，意作妙观三密相应。但是依照一般规定，必须经过上师贯顶，传授方可修习。又因受法机会颇难，所以只能靠个人因缘和机会才能得修。

其他类有印度的瑜伽、西方的催眠术等。

气者，何也？乃能量也。就是在意念（思想）的引导下调集体内的能量，以便做功、练功。能量是生命的动力，生物维持生命的过程就是新陈代谢的生化过程，需要消耗能量；人体脏器运动做功，需要消耗能量；体力劳动或脑力劳动更要消耗能量；"人活一口气"，"气"停止了，能量消耗完毕，生命亦即停止了，所以，能量是整个生命活动不可缺的东西。

在中国气功中，道教继承传统诸家气功功法，开辟了多种多样的气功入静法门。道教文献中所见的气功方法，有百数十种，既有静功，又有动功、动静功，而以静功为主。道教气功静功入静法，大略可分为炼神、炼气、存思、守窍、内丹五大类。

炼神类，此类方法源出老庄，从调心入手，以空虚心念、令契合于虚无之道为修习之要，有守道、守神、守一、心斋、定观、澄心、观心、坐忘、炼神还虚、炼神合道等名目。

炼神类功夫，与佛教有所相通。南北朝以来，道教在源于老庄的守道、守神说的基础上，吸收佛教天台止观及禅宗禅法，形成一类佛、道融合的炼神之道。《洞玄灵宝定观经》所说"定观"，实即佛教"止观"的改头换面。唐代所出的《三论元旨》，依"重玄"哲学，分炼神入定的阶次为"摄心归一"（安定）、"灰心忘一"（灭定）、"悟心真一"（泰定）三阶。初以一念摄万念，"内静观心，澄彼纷葩，归乎寂泊"，若心念浮躁难收，用"放心远观"之法，纵心远观四方无极世界，至无可观处，然后摄归，从头至足，观身体虚假无常。又可心依气息而观，或"怡神而已，精照一源"，由此达寂定不动。次"忘心遣观"，连寂定的心念也泯灭，使形同槁木，心若死灰，境智双忘，谓之"灰心忘一"。次由忘一而达真一，心与道合，因忘而明，因明而达，"悟心真一"，达《庄子》所云"宇泰定则发天光"的最高境界。

宋代以来，道教炼神之道还进一步与禅宗之禅融合，提倡明心见性，被称为内丹中的"上品丹法"、"最上一乘顿法"。

炼气类，此类方法源出先秦的吐纳食气、行气，以调制呼吸为主，有行气、闭气、胎息、吐纳、服气、食气等名目。修习大体分闭息、多入少出、服咽内元气、服食外气等法。

闭息，在《抱朴子·释滞》称"行炁"（炁，中药上指脐带）。方法是从鼻中吸气，然后闭而不呼，逐渐延长闭息时间，于闭息时默数数，从一数至一百二十，渐增至千。不可闭抑时，从口中微微吐气出。气之出入，皆须深细绵密。

多入少出的服气法，以调息令多入少出为要。如《太清调气经》云："鼻长引气，口满即咽，然后一吐，须少，每引须多。"方法是入五吐一及息入后闭停少时，呼时三分气中出二分，留一分，再停顿少时。

存服外气，为存思与服气的结合，有服五芽、六气、雾、三气、紫气等多种方法。五芽，指五方所生的五色气，道教认为外五气与内五脏五气相应，面向五方，存服五气，有补益脏气、健身延年之效。存服之法，据《太上养生胎息气经》等所说，先面东平坐握固，闭目叩齿三通，存想东方青气（青芽）入于我口，纳气服咽九次，以舌舐唇漱津咽下三次，存想青气入己肝脏中，氤氲盘旋，循行诸脉。次存服南方赤气（丹芽）、中央黄气（黄芽）、西方白气（素芽）、北方黑气（黑芽）。服三气法，是于日初出时，面向日，存想日下有青白赤三色气，直下入我口中，服咽其气九十度。服雾法，为存想有五色云气郁郁然，口纳其气服咽五十度。服紫气法为存想自己泥丸宫中有紫气出，勃勃冲天，采服此气。

存服内元气法之内元气，指吐气时从自己气海丹田中上升的气，当此气升入口中时，闭口连连鼓咽，想其声汩汩，直入气海。《幻真先生服内元气诀》等分其法为进取、淘气、调气、咽气、行气、炼气、委气、闭气、布气等十余诀，其中咽气指服咽内元气，行气指内元气咽下后，以意领气，从下丹田后穿夹脊，循脊柱上升至头顶，然后降下，遍行于毛发、头面、颈项、手臂、十指、五脏、两腿、足心，最后想周身病气瘀血被正气荡涤，从手足端散出，谓之"散气"。这种服气法再发展一步，便走向了内丹。

存思类，存思，略同佛教所谓"观想"，为持续想象某种形象之意，是符箓派道教主要的修炼方法，源出纬书。道教徒修炼时存思的对象，大体可分为具宗教内容者与不具宗教内容

静功

者两类。具宗教内容者，如身内外的神祇、仙境、天宫等，存思的神祇，有《太平经》所述五脏神、身中二十四神，《大洞真经》所言三十九神真，及日月、五星、北斗等神，而以存思身内三丹田中神真为主，《抱朴子》等名曰"守真一"。另有"三一九宫法""默朝上帝"等，以上丹田中被认为居主宰地位的太一帝君等神为存思对象。这类存思法渗透了有神论及飞升出世的宗教内容，但其修炼的过程，从客观上来看，无疑有气功的内核。

不具宗教内容的存思法，有内视法、存服日月光华法、服三色气法、服元气法、酥沐法、服紫霄法等。如《丹书紫字三五顺行经》述内视法为，端坐内视，存想自身中脏腑肠胃，了了分明，久行之能真内见脏腑。《紫度炎光经》所述内视法，为令耳目遥注于百里、千里之外。谓久行之能见闻远方之事，得遥视遥听之能。又如《云笈七签》卷四五"服日月芒法"，常存心中有日象大如铜钱，赤色九芒，从心中出喉，至口中，复返还于胃。存思良久，吐气咽津若干次。服月华法为存思脑中有月象，放白光，下照入喉，服咽其光。服元气法，乃存想空中元和之气郁然而下，如云如雨，流润自身，透皮肉，入骨髓，四肢五脏皆受其浸润，有如流水渗入地中。酥沐法，想象头顶有酥团融化，流注入脑，下溉心间，周行四肢。以上二法有补益虚损之特效。服三气、服云气、服紫霄等法，为存服赤白黑紫等各色气、光，有通过想象吸收外界生命能量的意味。

守窍类，此类方法以意守丹田为门径，有"守一""胎息""存神炼气"等名目。如唐代孙思邈《存神炼气铭》云："欲学此术，先须绝粒，安心气海，存神丹田，摄心静虑。"幻真先生《胎息经注》释"胎从伏气中结"云："修道者常伏气于脐下，守其神于身内，神气相合而生玄胎。"此类方法，入手门径与内丹基本相同。

除静功外，道教还继承发展先秦秦汉的导引、按摩术，辅以叩齿、咽津、鸣天鼓等，作为治病健身、益寿延年乃至成仙得道的重要方法。导引、按摩，以动摇肢体为法，最初相当简单，多模仿动物的姿势，如《抱朴子》所言"龙导虎引、熊经龟咽、燕飞蛇屈鸟伸、天俛地仰"等，五禽戏、八段锦等，皆属此类。这类锻炼方法，多与调息、闭气、冥思、存想结合，成为气功动功、动静功。其动作姿势，愈演愈繁，如司马承祯《服气精义论》所述导引法有数十式，与印度瑜伽体位法颇多相类。服气、叩齿、鸣天鼓相配合，动静相兼，成为道教气功功法的一大特色。

道教气功炼养，还往往与辟谷、服饵、房中术相配合。辟谷以进入气功态为基础，又被认为是气功功夫深湛的表现，或被作为进入气功态的手段。辟谷大多服药，服气、内丹等气功，也多服用药物以为辅助。道教的各种炼养之道，对房中术皆十分重视，房中术既包含有性生活方面的卫生知识，又有气功的内容，或被当作气功的修炼途径。

道教从养生健身、延寿成仙的宗旨出发，全面继承发展中华传统诸家的各种炼养方法，吸收外来佛教、印度教炼养学的精华，形成了自家多渠道、多层次的气功养生体系。较之以精神解脱为根本宗旨的佛教及以道德修养为根本立场的儒家，道教显然更长于养生，独具佛、儒二家所缺的动功、辟谷、服饵、房中等术，具动静兼备、内外结合的特点。较之以治病为根本宗旨的医家以及技击为根本宗旨的武术气功，道教气功更富高层次的功法及精深系统的理论。在中国封建社会的儒释道等诸家中，道教被公认最擅长于养生，以儒治世，以佛治心，以道治身。

道教气功的功法，除具宗教性内容的存思神真一类外，其他方法，从客观方面看来，都很少或不具宗教内容，只要修习者不带有长生成仙的信仰，完全可以视之为气功。

PART 1

Splendid Chinese Cuisine
—— Thriving Chinese Cuisine Culture

"Cuisine and conjugal life are desires of people. "

Traditionally, the Chinese ancestors and sages had a conservative attitude toward sex, but channeled their desires to cuisine. Therefore, in China, cuisine not only has developed highly, but also has a great social importance.

In the first place, customarily, in important events, such as wedding, etc. , feasting is often an indispensable arrangement. Secondly, cuisine is an important means in social life. When a good friend comes from a remote place, he is entertained with cuisine. In the ancient time, administration of the state was described as "administering the tripods and quadripod" , a typical term in cookery, which reflected the high standing of Chinese cuisine.

Chinese people are expert at eating. They eat all kinds of animals. They also eat certain animal's viscera that the Westerners do not eat. They consider that liver is nutrimental for blood; kidney is nutrimental for kidney; etc. They consider petrel's nest, bear's palm, leopard's foetus, phoenix' (eagle's) marrow, dragon's (snake's) gall bladder, horse's genitals, elephant's nose, shark's fin and gorilla's lips all as rare delicacies. People in Guangdong Province eat baked cicadas and roasted beetles at restaurants. In a word, the catalogue of delicious foods is very extensive.

In addition, Chinese people eat a lot of vegetable dishes, which are prepared often as meat dishes. In the Chinese vegetable restaurants, you can discover on the menu"vegetable pig's kidney", "vegetable pig's intestines" "vegetable fish" , etc. These are mostly bean products. Bean curd is welcomed by all the people, rich or poor. Soy sauce is a Chinese industry, which is a delicious, appetizing and nutritious condiment. Soy sauce manufacture is a great contribution to nutrition and health.

however, western cuisines put great emphasis on the scientific collocations of nutrition, Chinese cuisine also expresses artistic pursuits not merely for the satisfying of stomach, but a creative art. The arrangement of the tableware is not a simple matter. It has to be done artistically. Well-off families often keep several sets of tableware. Since the Tang-Song Dynasties, Chinese teahouses and restaurants are usually located by riverside and housed in a garden architecture, providing their patrons with extra delight. Even the names of dishes are delightful. For example, a soup with floating peas is named; "a flying white egret in the blue sky," rather poetically. Other examples are "emerald chicken soup" , "jade frog legs" "duck webs amidst flowers" , and "braised dragon, tiger and phoenix" , all combine literature with appetite.

The Chinese cuisine demands the "complete presence of color, fragrance and taste". "Color" refers not to the colors each ingredi-

Pear Salad

ent displays to the visual effects of combinations of different colors in food modelling of foods. Foods are often carved by the chef into various artistic designs. It was recorded that in the region of Bai Yue (now Guangdong Province) there were two dishes designed so artistically that named "watching dishes". They can be both watched and eaten, but chiefly for watching. Their modelling is often

Pan—Fried Buns

Cured Fish

exquisite with symbolic meanings. For example, a fish dish symbolizes "surplus" (In Chinese language, "fish" and "surplus" both are pronounced "yu"). In the Qing Dynasty, foods were often arranged like words with auspicious meaning, particularly at banquets in palaces and noble families. The emphasis over "color" reflects that Chinese people

Hand—Made Tofu

are very attentive to the appearance and forms of cuisines.

"Fragrance" refers to the fragrant and appetizing smell of the dishes served on the table before eating. Even in earlier days the Chinese people had already mastered skills to use spices to prepare strongly fragrant dishes. Most Chinese kitchens are oily and smoky and hard to be cleaned, but fragrance issued from the kitchens are often welcome to passers-by. Poets often praised home dishes. They wrote poems praising foods in their home towns, e. g., the "bass, asparagus and watershield soup".

"Taste" refers to the taste of food. The Chinese do not care for the nutrition in food as much as its taste. For instance, the westerners throw away chicken feet along with bones and feather; the Chinese enjoy eating chicken feet for its special taste. The ancient Chinese dramatist Li

Liweng nicknamed himself "crab slave" , because he savored crabs attentively. Savoring foods is important for the Chinese. A gourmet can find out slight differences in the tastes. The Chinese gourmets are this qualification. The Chinese maybe lazy in preparing dishes is the last thing that Chinese will show a lazy attitude to.

Since ancient times, the Chinese have employed many cooking methods, such as braising, boiling, braising with soy sauce, roasting, baking, grilling, scalding, deep-frying, steaming, drying, salt-preserving, etc. *Cardinal Techniques for Uniting the People* written in the Qi State listed approximately one hundred different dishes and the meth-

Durian Tarts

ods for preparing them, including twenty grilling methods. Some foods are grilled inside a short bamboo pole. Some foods are first covered with mud and then grilled.

According to the Chinese traditional medicine, food can be classified into four categories by their nature different foods, and divided them into four categories of cool, warm, hot and moderate. Hot and warm foods generate heat, expel coldness, warm up the viscera and smoothen the channels. Cool foods reduce heat, detoxify and tranquilize. The effects of moderate food are between between the hot and the cool. Knowledge of the properties of foods is contributory to disease treatment and health care. For instance, eating hot foods, such as mutton and goat meat, in winter, helps resist coldness. Eating cool foods, such as watermelon and mung bean, in summer, helps relieving

Steamed Crab

Hot pot

heat.

Different seasons suit different tastes. "Spring suits sour taste; summer suits bitter taste; autumn suits pungent taste; winter suits salty taste. " (*Book of Rites:Internal Rules*) Spring witnesses the sprouting of plants, the easy contamination of foods by bacteria, and the unstable weather. Appetite can be hindered. It is desirable to eat sour foods so as to kill bacteria and stimulate appetite. In summer, eating too much meat induces acid reaction in the stomach. Much water is consumed and mouth is apt to be dry. Eating bitter gourd or drinking leaf mustard soup has a refreshing, cooling effect. Autumn is cool. It is desirable to eat foods that are sweet and somewhat pungent, with a fair amount of calories. Winter is cold. It is desirable to eat meat with a large amount of calories and salty food. Salt reacts with stomach acid to form hydrochloric acid, helpful for digesting meat. The above sums up the desirable tastes for the four seasons, meeting the demands of physiologic-physics and physiologic-chemistry.

Chinese food therapy combines Chinese medicine and cuisine. The first Chinese medical code, *Yellow Emperor's Canon of Internal Medi-*

Seafood in Cantonese Style

cine, points out: "Noxious matter impairs health. Five grains preserve health. Five fruits help preserve health. Five livestock meats improve health. Five spices are also helpful. " That is to say, foods and medicine should be combined in treating diseases. There are two kinds of medicinal foods. One kind are pure foods, used to improve health and looks. Among such foods are cherry, which is sweet and moderate and improves vigor and looks; tangerine, which eliminates mouth odour, invigorates the body and leads to a slim build and longer life; date, which reinforces energy and leads to a slim build and longer life; watermelon seeds, which are sweet and moderately cool, and improve looks; bamboo shoots, which quench the thirst, facilitate urination and increase vigor; ginger, which stops bleeding, prompts sweating and dispels cold and moisture. The other kind of medicinal foods are foods for curing diseases in combination with medicine. Among such foods are gingseng, donkey hide gelatin, orange skin, poria coccus, peony root bark, and rehmannia glutinosa. There are numerous foods of this kind, which are fairly effective in curing diseases. Many folk prescriptions make use of such foods. As an old saying goes: "Thirty percent therapy and seventy percent nutrition. "

Chinese cuisine culture has been very thriving, in both quality and quantity. According to a historical record, in the Southern Song Dynasty, when Zhang Jun, a general, entertained Emperor Gao at a sumptuous banquet, 102 dishes were served in addition to 120 plates of desserts and refreshments. The banquet lasted from morning to night. The so-called "full Manchu-Han banquet" in the Qing Dynasty included 100 dishes of delicious foods from the north and south of China in addition to forty to fifty plates of light refreshments, and ten to twenty plates of nuts, fruits and pickles, and lasted a whole day. This reflects the attitude of the Chinese towards foods, with their inclination for sumptuousness. In general, Chinese housewives can cook some particular delicious dishes. As a saying goes: "When a husband's stomach is contented, so is his mind."

① Four Major Groups of Chinese Cuisine

The Chinese cuisine is divided into four major groups, based on the localities of their origin. (Of course, they can be subdivided into numerous subgroups). The four major groups are: Su (Suzhou, Yangzhou and Hangzhou) group, Yue (Guangdong) group, Chuan (Sichuan) group and Lu (Shandong) group. Below is a brief introduction to their features.

A. Yue (Guangdong) Cuisine

Yue Cuisine made its debut in Canton. It is characterized firstly by its wide and strict selection of ingredients. Seafood and game food are the first-rate courses. Besides chicken, duck and goose, pigeon, partridge and quail also make delectable dishes. For seafood, the Cantonese take to grouper, pomfret, hairtail, conger eel, turtle, prawn and crab. Their favorite game foods include reptiles and amphibians; terrapin, pangolin, tortoise and snake. Yue Cuisine holds fastidious norms in selecting ingredients. For instance, for white cut chicken, they require Qingyuan (county) chicken and Wenchang (county) chicken. For other dishes, they select mouse-speckled grouper, silver pomfret, off-shore prawn, gold-stained tortoise and blackmane goose as superior ingredients.

Secondly, Guangdong people favor light, delicious, refreshing and slippery tastes. Their cooking methods are mostly steaming, saute and stir-frying with thick gravy. Due to the long duration of summer, they favor light and refreshing foods and aquatic food. They like to taste the original flavor of sea foods and fresh foods. Only in winter do they eat fatty foods and strongly flavored foods, such as dog's meat, stewed pork chunks, fried oyster, braised eel, pig's knuckle, etc.

The third characteristic of Guangdong cuisine is plenty of supportive vegetables, due to the substantial scope of local produce. In

Stir—Fried Prawns Stuffed with Vermicelli

the north of Guangdong are grown plenty of mushrooms and bamboo shoots. With the favorable climate, the province abounds also in rich varieties of fruits, such as pineapple, litchi, plum, cocoa nut, banana, Chinese chestnut, etc. All these can make hygienic dishes.

The fourth characteristic is the many kinds of porridge and refreshments. The long summer and a lot of perspiration require meat porridge to replenish the nutriments and water lost. Porridge shops (including some canteens affiliated to "five or four-star" hotels) prepare a stock of base porridge (called "taste porridge") with ingredients of hens, pig's bones, dried scallops and soybean rolls. When a customer asks for a certain kind of porridge,

Crispy Duck

Chitterlings in Soy Sauce

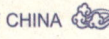

the cook adds to the base porridge some other suitable, ready-made ingredients such as fish, shrimp, crab, frog, meat ball, pig's giblets, beef, chicken, duckling, etc. , as well as ginger, Chinese onion and pepper

Duck Blood Curd Stewed in Chilli Sauce, Accompanied with Ham, Tripe, Bean Sprouts, Coriander Leaves, and Shallots

Vermicelli Mixed with Sichuan Pepper and Chilli Dil

powder. Located at the junction of international exchanges, Guangzhou has amalgamated both the overseas and domestic merits in preparing refreshments. Every teahouse or hotel provides hundreds of cakes and refreshments.

B. Chuan (Sichuan) Cuisine

Chuan Cuisine traces back to the ancient Ba Kingdom (modern Chongqing) and Shu Kingdom (modern Chengdu) and is remarkable for its oily and hot taste. This is due to the foggy, cloudy and damp climate in the Sichuan Basin. Hot food is useful for dispersing dampness. Sichuan folks are keen for hot oxen's giblet pot, hot beancurd and other hot foods.

Another characteristic of the Chuan cuisine is its preparation of different dishes with the same raw material. With a piece of half-fat, half-lean pork, Sichuan cooks can prepare a number of different dishes with different flavors, such as salted-fried pork slices, re-cooked pork slices, sweet and hot shredded pork, fried pork cubes, sliced pork cooked with rice crust, sweet steamed pork chunks, salty steamed pork chunks, pork steamed with ground glutinous rice, white cut hot pork, etc.

The third charcteristic of the Sichuan cuisine is the tasty snacks, including hot ox-head meat, spiced chicken, tea-stewed ducking, marinated rabbit meat, pickled vegetables, dumplings, eight-treasure rice puddings, etc.

C. Lu (Shandong) Cuisine

Lu Cuisine, also called Qi and Lu Cuisine, originated from Linzi and Qufu, respectively the capitals of ancient Qi State and Lu State. It has traces of palatial cuisine. Its first characteristic is its strongly flavored dishes made of costly ingredients such as petrel nest, shark fin, abalone, fish tripe, sea cucumber, deer meat, mushrooms, white fungus, clam, etc.

Due to the long duration of the cold weather in north China and shortage of vegetables, the cooks in Shandong are skilled in making high-heat and high-protein dishes. It is the second characteristic of the Lu cuisine. Typical Shandong delicacies are: skin-crisp roasted duck, nine-bends pig intestines, bone-detached braised chicken, in-wok-fried Yellow River carp, conch braised in soy sauce, and deep-fried oyster.

Lu cuisine cooks used to keep a wok of flavoring broth (with old hen and pig knuckles, etc. , as ingredients) and sprinkle it into the pan as a substitute for gourmet powder. It is the third characteristic as well as a tradition of the Lu cuisine. The Lu cuisine cooks are also expert at preparing milk soups. The vegetable milk soup in Jinan has enjoyed a fame.

D. Su Cuisine

Su Cuisine originated from Suzhou, and later from Yangzhou and Hangzhou too. Its first characteristic is the combination of relishes of both the Southerners and the Northerners. This region was the abode of the emperors during the Six-Dynasties and the Southern Song Dynasty. The Great Canal flowing through the region has facilitated the exchanges between the South and the North. The Su cuisine chefs, on the one hand are dexterous in cooking southern style dishes, which are tasty and refreshing, and on the other hand are dexterous in cooking high-heat and high-protein dishes, such as stewed pig knuckles with ham, braised "Lion's Head" (pork balls) and stir-fried eel pastry. In the

Minced Meatball, Nicknamed Lion's Head

Deep-Fried Mandarin Fish in Sweet and Sour Sance

menu of the Su cuisine can be found a long list of dishes suiting both the Southerners and the Northerners.

Plenty of lake produce and seafood constitute the second characteristic of the Su cuisine. Such dishes include the Crab-yellow Lion's

Head, Crab-yellow petrel nest, Shark fin in shrimp soup, West-Lake sweet sour fish, Steamed hilsa herring (produced in the Fuchun River), meat-stuffed lotus root, spicy Tai-Lake crucian carp soup, lotus-seed duck broth, etc.

The third characteristic of the Su cuisine is its exquisite refreshments and snacks, such as Pine-nut-crystalline-meat sweet cake, Crab-yellow-soup bun, Crab-yellow steamed dumpling, Ningbo dumpling, etc., which are famed throughout China.

Tea Utensils

Etiquette of Tea Culture

② Tea Culture

Tea is the traditional beverage of the Chinese people. The Chinese people were the earliest in the world to plant and drink tea. A saying goes "The seven first things in the morning are: Faggot, rice, oil, salt, soy sauce, tea and vinegar", that shows the place of tea in the everyday life of the Chinese.

It is said that Shen Nong discovered tea in wild mountains in remote antiquity, "Shen Nong used to taste hundreds of herbs for medical purposes. One day he tasted seventy-two poisonous herbs, but with the aid of tea he was detoxified." At first, tea was used as an antidotal medicine. Then it was found to be able to relieve internal heat and invigorate mind, and people began to use it as a beverage. Tea drinking became a vogue that has lasted over two thousand years. The Chinese started to drink tea at about the same time as the Egyptians built the pyramids. With a long history of tea drinking, tea culture was representative of the spiritual pursuits of the ancient Chinese culture. It was a symbol of the Chinese culture.

Tea is grown in beautiful hills absorbing the sweet dews and the essence of Heaven and Earth! The ancient Chinese attributed to it the personalities of lofty people. First, they exacted suitable surroundings for enjoying it. Indoors, the surroundings should consist of a clean courtyard or quiet room. Outdoors, the surroundings should be sunny in the day with gentle breezes, or moonlit in the night with gentle breezes. Wen Zhenheng, a scholar in the Ming Dynasty, declared in his work

Etiquette of Tea Culture

A Set of Tea Utensils

Book on Surpluses: "A hut should be built on the hillside, with a young servant to make tea. So, the host may converse with friends all day long or sit alone all night. " He considered it to be of primary importance to a "secluded man". Rich people used to set a tea-room in his residence. Scholars liked rather to sip tea in hills and woods. The following poem is a description of such surroundings:

Where does tea steam rise?

One wonders at a fishing boat lying to the west of the bamboo grove.

At the silent foot of the Southern Hill,

Tea steam rises out of the woods.

People in such surroundings may live a simple life with high ideals.

Tea cannot be made without water. Tea lovers of every generation seek for high-quality water. Lu Yu, the author of *Canon of Tea* that is alleged to be the first work on tea in the world, devoted a whole chapter to discussing how to get high-quality water. He stated that the best water for making tea is water in springs on hills. The next choice is water in rivers. The last choice is water in wells. Many later scholars also wrote books on choices of water for making tea. In the Qing Dynasty, wherever Emperor Qianlong went, he always ordered the followers to search for springs. Then he tried the samples and graded them. He ranked the Jade Spring the first. The next ones were the Yixun Spring north of the Great Wall, the Pearl Spring in Ji'nan, the Gold Hill Spring on the Yangtze River. . . The norms of grading the water are: deliciousness, freshness and sweetness. Some ancient Chinese also used rainwater, ice water, dew water and snow water to make tea, firstly because of their freshness and deliciousness, secondly because of the delightful interest they induced. In *Dream of Red Mansion*, Lady Miao Yu, who was an expert in savoring tea, collected snow flakes on plum blossoms, buried the snow flakes under the earth for five years, and then used the dissolved water to make tea. Of course, the ordinary people cannot afford to do so.

Etiquette of Tea Culture

Du Kang, the Legendary Inventor of Chinese Wine

The fire for boiling the water for making tea also involves much care. Boiling the water with wood will cause the water to taste slightly of the wood. It is best to use charcoal. Ancient Chinese called charcoal fire "active fire", firstly because it was without smoke, secondly because it burnt vigorously. As stated by Su Shi, a poet in the Song Dynasty, "Delicious water needs active fire."

Watching boiling water was a meticulous procedure since the Tang-Song Dynasties. People in the Tang Dynasty used a "cauldron" (a vessel) with an open mouth for observing to what degree the water had been boiled. Tea brewed with over boiled water loses its flavor. Lu Yu divided the boiling into three states: "At the first state of boiling, the bubbles are like fish eyes, and the water issues a light sound. At the second state of boiling, water around the rim of the vessel spurts like a chain of pearls. At the third state of boiling, water is very wavy." There

Shaoxing Yellow Wine

were different opinions as to which was the best state. The Song scholars thought that water was best for making tea just after the second state. Perhaps this opinion is reasonable.

The overall art of savoring tea is also related to the vessels used. Feng Zhengqing said in his book *Remarks on Tea*, that each drinker should use a small tea pot and pour tea into a cup himself, for the fragrance of tea lasts only a short moment after it is brewed. The fragrance would not be present when the tea is sipped early, and would be lost when the tea is sipped late. The model, color and quality of the tea set also matter. Lu Yu liked Yuezhou celadon, because the color of celadon and the color of tea are harmonious. But Cai Xiang in the Song Dynasty said that "a light color tea decoction should use a black tea set" to get the contrasting beauty. Different aesthetic interests led to different views. It was said that "the best tea set cost 100, 000 coins" in the Ming Dynasty. This shows how highly the ancient Chinese valued the tea sets.

Tea may be sipped alone or be used to entertain friends and guests. Sipping tea alone requires a pleasant and relaxed mood and quiet surroundings. According to *Commentaries on Tea* written by Xu Cishu: "When there are a large number of guests, they should be entertained with wine. A new, casual acquaintance should be entertained with fruit. Only when the guest is a close friend whom you could talk and argue

Hometown of Shaoxing Yellow Wine

with freely, should you light fire, boil water and brew tea for entertainment. How much tea would be brewed depends on the number of guests. One pot of boiling water would suffice three persons or less. Two pots would suffice five or six. When there were too many guests, tea would not be used to entertain them. " When several friends drink tea together, serenity is also necessary.

In fine, among all peoples in the world, the attitude of the Chinese toward tea is unique. They emphasize a lofty and leisurely mood, quiet and fine surroundings, freshness and clearness of water, elegant tea sets and close, good friends entertained. In tasting tea, although the Chinese take a great delight in its brewing, yet their real purpose is to achieve spiritual ascendancy. So, tea is not just for satisfying the taste, but is a part of life.

③ Wine Culture

China stands out as one of the pioneering nations in wine brewing in the world. According to *Stratagems of Warring States*, the initiator of wine was Yi Di in the Xia Dynasty; According to *Analysis of Words*, the initiators of wine were Yi Di and Du Kang in the Zhou Dynasty. The ancient Chinese often used "Du Kang" as a synonym of wine. For instance, Cao Cao said in a poem of him, "What relieves my worries? Only Du Kang does. "

Wine has been considered as a special culture in China. Poor people and rich people both drink wine. To describe the excessive extravagance of the nobles, it was said,"wine fills a pool; meat forms a forest";

and "wine and meat decay inside the vermilion door. " sending off an army on expedition or celebrating triumph, wedding, anniversary or alliance treaties signing ceremonies, wine is always present. On occasions of tomb sweeping, wine is sprinkled at the front and on the top of tombs in honor of the deceased. In ancient times, when people practised divination, prayed for rainfall, or worshipped deities and ghosts, wine was often used to show reverence. Even when a prisoner was taken off to be executed, he was offered a bowl of wine. On all solemn occasions wine is not replaceable by tea. In the eyes of the Chinese people wine has a special place.

There are many kinds of wine. In terms of brewing time, there are spring wine, hundred-day wine, overnight wine, etc. In terms of raw materials, there are rice wine, wheat wine, oats wine, red sorghum wine, wild pepper wine, grape wine, chrysanthemum wine, plum wine, osmanthus wine, elm wine, horse-milk wine, etc. Grape wine is brewed with fresh or dry grapes, and was disseminated to Central China from the Western Region. Chrysanthemum wine, plum wine, and osmanthus wine are brewed from a mixture of grain and the flowers and stalks of the plants. People in different parts of China prefer different kinds of wine. The southerners prefer yellow wine. Yellow wine is a unique Chinese wine and one of the oldest wines in the world. It originated in the Xia-Shang Dynasties, and is also called old wine. The Yellow Wine brewed in Shaoxing is the most renowned yellow wine. The northerners prefer white liquor. White liquor is a traditional Chinese wine. In terms of processes of fermentation, white liquor can be divided into solid-fermented liquor, liquid-fermented liquor and semi-solid-fermented liquor. In terms of the yeasts, white liquor can be divided into big yeast liquor, small yeast liquor and bran-yeast liquor. In terms of fragrance, white liquor can be divided into delicate fragrance liquor, soy fragrance liquor, strong fragrance liquor, rice fragrance liquor, etc. Sorghum white liquor is most liked by the northern. It symbolizes their courage and strong sentiments.

Medicinal liquor, too, has a long history in China. It was said: "Liquor is the chief medicine. " Liquor itself is good for dispersing chills and improving blood circulation. When Hua Tuo performed surgery, he mixed anaesthetic powder with wine to relieve the pain of the patient. Medicine is added to a liquor to increase its curing effect. Examples are: snake wine for treating rheumatism, ginseng wine for postponing

The Finger-Guessing Game When Having Chinese Liquor

aging, three-genitals (of deer, ox and horse) wine for consolidating masculinity, tiger-bone wine for treating bone injuries, etc. In *Syllabus of Medical Herbs* are listed scores of recipes of medical wine. Adding valuable medicines into wine is a Chinese speciality.

As early as in the Han Dynasty there were wineshop streets in cities. In *Biographies of Knight-Errants of the History of Han*, it was recorded:"The two patrons of wineshops Zhao Jundu and Jia Ziguang were both renowned gallant people in Changan who took up revenges and assassinations." In the "Records on Buddhism in Luoyang; Fayan Temple" written in the Southern-Northern Dynasties, it was recorded: "In the west of the city there were two lanes called the Wine-Selling Lane and the Wine-Drinking Lane, The residents in the two lanes did mostly the wine-brewing business. " Both records denote the existence of wine shops in ancient times. In order to attract customers, the wine shops hung in front of the shops yellow triangular flag painted with the Chinese character for wine, "酒". Master Han Fei wrote;"In the state of Song, wine sellers hang wine flags high up." Wine flags were the earliest mentioned advertisement. The ancient Chinese regarded delicious wine on a par with beautiful women. There were legends about beautiful women in a wine shop. For example, there were the legends of "Lady Zhuo Wenjun at wineshop counter" and "the northern tribal lady at wineshop counter" , etc.

Wine has dual properties. On the one hand, it makes the drinker bold and militant. As described in a Tang poem:"In a luminous cup, grape wine is sweet. As I am drinking it, the lute sounds press me to mount my steed. " On the other hand, it renders the drinker pessimistic and downcast, and renders the sober and cynical drinker lethargic and sleepy. As described by a saying, "To drown sorrow in wine makes one even more sorrowful. " What is more, excessive drinking results in quarrels, conflicts and even fatal accidents. The ancient Chinese said, "There are four vices in life: wine, amour, fortune, and temper. " Wine ranks the first of the four vices. Addicts to wine and amour are designated debauchers.

Although drunkenness makes people act like a buffoon and talk nonsense, yet Chinese hosts at feasts used to urge their guests to drink wine until they are drunken. It contrasts with the Western courtesy. This phenomenon has two implications:

A. One is to show the generosity and hospitality of the host. The more the host urges his guest to drink wine, the more generous and hospitable he is. Normally the Chinese are thrifty, but they are apt to be extravagant at feasts.

B. Drinking wine beyond a limit would cause drunkenness. Usually the Chinese are quiet and polite. When they drink wine together, they are often noisy and often play finger-guessing games. Thus they divulge their suppressed feelings. It is another aspect of their life.

How to make people drink more wine?"To refuse a toast but to drink the wine as a penalty," is a clause used to satirize someone who does not distinguish between a good will and a bad will. But at the dinner table it is solely for urging people to drink more wine. The wine drinking penalty rule is then for compelling and justifying people to drink more wine cheerfully, and is imbued with hospitality and good will. From this we may detect a cultural phenomenon reflecting the pleasure of jokes and games.

There are many ways of wine drinking penalties. Some ways are scholarly and dependent on wit; for example, "practising wine orders". In this game, someone is made the commander and others must obey his orders at the table, either to compose a poem or do some other things. The person who fails to carry out the order is penalized to drink. This game is practised among the upper-class people. In *Dream of Red Mansion*, the clever ladies often did it at the table to enhance pleasure.

Other ways are coarse and straightforward, for example, "finger-guessing". This is an exclusive game in China. It is said to be practised also in Japan, but is imported from China. There are many series of watchwords in the game, different in different localities, but all cling to the ten-numerals from one to ten. The guest stretches some fingers and says a number. The other guest also stretches out some fingers and says a number. When the number of all the stretched fingers corresponds with the number he says, he wins and the other guest loses. And vice versa. The loser is penalized to drink wine. The guests usually get more and more vehement and noisy as if quarreling. In the din, the winner is pleased. If the loser tries to avoid taking the penalty, he will be laughed at by others at the table, but all are done with a good will. Thus, drinking wine becomes an amusement and a pleasure.

Yet some other ways depend more on chance, reflecting the Chinese view on fatalism. Such examples are: "floating a cup on a winding pool", and "Beating drum and passing flower. " Due to the unpredictable water flow, the cup may stop anywhere in front of anybody. The person in front of whom the cup stops has to drink the cup of wine as a penalty: Similarly, the flower may be passed on while the drum is being beaten, but as soon as the beating stops, the passing must stop. Whoever still holding the flower in his hand is penalized to drink wine. Because of the unpredictability, the participants are all the time very intense, which brings about fun.

To sum up, wine and tea represent almost all the ideals and pursuits of the Chinese people. Wine makes people congenial and inspires their worldly desires. Tea is cleansing and it stops such desires. Wine relates to rashness. Tea relates to soberness. When a person drinks wine, he is often unrestrained and wishes to make great contributions. When a person drinks tea, he is often restrained and only wishes to maintain his own integrity. With wine, drinking unrestrainedly represents fervency; and capacity for wine represents style. With tea, one is gentle and courteous, modest and deferential.

PART 2

Exercise of Bones, Muscles, Vitality and Breath

—— Chinese Martial Arts Designed to Improve Vitality

Chinese martial arts, also known as national martial arts, are a form of physical culture in China, that combined movements of kicking, hitting, wrestling, seizing, tumbling, striking, chopping and piercing into serial or single exercises, bare-handed or with weapons.

Chinese martial arts could trace back to the primeval society, when people used sticks, bars and other tools to struggle against beasts. Later, more effective weapons were made for struggles against beasts, etc. Earlier, martial arts were exercised only in the army, and later were exercised also by the common people. Martial arts developed greatly in the Ming Dynasty, when many schools of martial arts arose, together with theoretical books. Such books included theoretical conclusions.

Wudang Fist

The representative of them were *Jinong Faggot Book*, *On Martial Arts*, *Martial Arts Exercises After Farming*, etc. They registered the martial arts of the different schools with appendixes of mnemonic formulas and illustrations. They have been important materials for researches on martial arts.

The modern martial arts consist of three categories; the boxing (Long Boxing, Taiji Boxing, South Boxing, Form Boxing, Eight-Trigram Boxing, etc.); the weapon exercise (with long weapons, short weapons, soft weapons) ; and the sparring exercise (bare-handed or with weapons). The martial arts have been created and developed by the Chinese people and are a precious national cultural legacy.

1 Marrow of Chinese Martial Arts

With vigorous, graceful and somewhat laborious movements, Chinese martial arts provide the exercisers with beauty and strength. The persistent exercise will build up their body and strength. Martial arts involve methods and skills for fighting. They incorporate highly practical consecutive movements including jumping, falling, passing through, somersaulting, retreating, shaking, turning, kicking, hitting,wrestling, seizing, etc.

The consecutive movements should be done in close sequences so as to overcome the movements of the opponent. Any slight neglect in the gestures of hands, legs and body and in the timing will result in favoring the opponent. So, the Chinese martial arts emphasize the gestures and timing.

To attain the true essence, the Chinese martial arts stress guidance by masters, and conscientious practice. The exerciser should practise diligently until he can carry out the movements unhesitatingly and very naturally.

The Chinese martial arts stress perfection. From the angle of the art of attack and defence, there are three grades of martial arts: The inferior-grade exerciser does not master the arts at all. The middle-grade exerciser is skilled in the art, and concentrates his attentions in fighting. The senior-grade exerciser has a high degree of dexterity and carries out his movements very naturally to beat the opponent. His arts attain perfection.

All Chinese martial arts exercisers must learn shadow boxing. There are now 192 boxing schools with detailed historical origins, comparatively complete theoretical grounds and technical systems. They were categorized either according to the different mountains where they originated (e. g. Shaoling School from Shaoling Temple on Mount Song and Wudang School from Mount Wudang), or according to the different river basins where they originated (e. g. the Yangtze River Basin School and the Yellow River Basin School), or according to whether the boxing exercise were intended to train internal vitality or external dexterity, etc. Mainly there are the following schools: Long Boxing, Taiji Boxing, South Boxing, Form Boxing, Eight-Trigram Boxing, Backbone Boxing, Somersault Boxing, Trotting Boxing, "Chopping Snatching Boxing, Grasshopper Boxing, Eight-Extreme Boxing, Monkey Boxing, Drunkard Boxing, Showy Boxing, Fancy Boxing, Hawk-Claw Boxing, Sponge Boxing, Six-Harmony Boxing, Snake Boxing,

Intention Boxing, Teenager Boxing, Zha Boxing, etc.

The Eight-Trigram Boxing, originally named Palm Turning Boxing, Body Shifting Eight Trigram Boxing and Interlocked Eight Trigram Boxing, is characterized by changing positions of the palms and changing paces, somewhat resembling the Eight Trigrams in the *Book of Changes*. Its fighting principle is the "combination of attack and defense". It stresses the stratagem: "I move before my opponent moves, halt before my opponent halts; when my opponent attacks, I defend; when my opponent exhausts himself, I keep energetic; when my opponent retreats, I advance; when my opponent moves, I watch my opponent while he is moving, and discover and make use of opportunities;

Martial Arts from Shaolin

when my opponent is near, I attack him; I extricate myself and then attack my opponent, and while my opponent is not moving, I move. " In fine, the stratagem prefers sidewise attack to frontal assailant.

The Eight-Extreme Boxing has the full name of "Open the Door Eight-Extreme Boxing" and another name of "Mount-Yue-Eight-Extreme Boxing". Open the Door means the six methods of breaking open the opponent's "door" (defense posture). This boxing is called "Eight-Extreme", because there was an ancient assumption that "Beyond the nine continents exist eight Yin; beyond the eight Yin exist eight enormities; beyond the eight enormities exist eight extremes", indicating a very far-away place. It is called "Mount Yue", because it is alleged that it originated from Mount Yue Temple in Jiaozuo city of Henan Province.

The core of the technique of the Eight-Extreme Boxing comprises the Six Openings and the Eight Moves, viz., the Eight Extreme Defence, the Eight Extreme Hitting, the Six Elbowing, the Eight Extreme Firmness, the New Eight Extreme Defence, and the Eight Extreme Double tracks; and the six-direction confrontations with weapon. Power is exerted for bursting, shaking, breaking in, hitting, approaching, stabbing, squeezing, leaning, bumping and twining. It is characterized by concise, alternative long and short swift, bumping and twining moves, repeated elbowing and firm foothold. After the founding of the People's Republic of China, with the development of martial arts, it has been listed as a national athletic event.

The White-Eyebrow Boxing, a branch of the South Boxing, is believed to be initiated by a white-eyebrow monk in Mount Emei of

Sichuan Province. It is now prevailing in Sichuan, Guangdong, Hong Kong and Macao. It is characterized by ferociousness, coherence and wide range. Its hitting moves include whip hitting, double bump hitting and sharp arrow hitting. Its bridging moves include short quick bridging, worming bridging, checking bridging and closing bridging. Its kicking moves include sidewise punting and treading. Its series of boxing moves include the Small-Cross, the Big-Cross, the Three, Six and Eight Trigrams, the Eighteen Bridging, the Tiger Rushing out of the Jungle, etc.

The Shaolin Boxing is the representative boxing of the Long Box-

Shaolin Kicking

ing. In a broad sense, Shaolin Boxing refers to the broader Shaolin School. In a narrow sense, it refers to the boxing practised by the monks in the Shaolin Temple on Mount Song of Henan Province, including the exercise with weapons. In the Qing Dynasty the monks of Shaolin Temple taught publicly Muscle Changing Exercise, Eight Part Exercise, breathing exercise and some traditional gymnastics. From the turn of the Ming Dynasty to the reign of Emperor Xianfeng in the Qing Dynasty, the Shaolin Boxing combined External Dexterity and Inner Vigor. In the modern time, the Shaolin Boxing embodies the art of a Buddhist and is characterized by sturdiness, fast attacks, and coordinated forward and backward moves. Its serial moves are mostly short and straight. For the postures, it requires to keep the head upright and the eyes focussing on one point, and to take care of the upper, lower, left and right sides. It requires to stick out the chest and straighten the waist and to bend the knees and close slightly the toes. The knees should not be extended and the shoulders should not be stressed. While hitting out, the arms should neither be bent nor very straight, so as to defend while attacking and to attack while defending. While moving, gravity should be controlled. Actions should be nimble and stopping should be stable. Legs should be kept low while advancing, and high while retreating. The whole body should be coordinated in making moves. Stepping and striking should be swift. It has many series of moves, such as Minor Hong Boxing, Major Hong Boxing, Elder Hong Boxing, Arhat Boxing, Zhao Yang Boxing, Plum Boxing, Cannon Boxing, Seven-Star Boxing, Tender Boxing, etc. The series of sparring include Six-Directions Hand Twisting, Six-Directions Hand Gripping, Six-Directions Ear grasping, and Six-Directions Kicking and Hitting, etc. In addition, there are some separate series of moves for practising, including Heart-Mind Moves, etc.

Cha Boxing, otherwise named "Fork Boxing" or "Inserting Boxing", is so named, because its moves are largely "zha" (finger thrusting). It has three characteristics: Firstly, it has a clear rhythm. Secondly, its moves are coherent, starting quickly and halting stably. Thirdly, it exerts force with momentum, It requires "to stride like wind, stand like a nail, rise like an ape, and fall like an eagle. " Moving should be as a

Performing Taiji

fierce tiger, stopping should be firm as a mountain. The moves should be swift, unhurried, staunch yet nimble. The sequences should be clear-cut, with sudden turning and stopping. Whether attacking or defending, advancing or retreating, the sequences should be fast but not disorderly, slow but coherent. The postures should be proper. Actions should be coordinated. The ten keys for the action are shrinking, minimizing, twining, soft, cunning, missing, speeding, firm, direct and sliding. The hand actions include thrusting, tantalizing, splitting, covering, picking, embracing, inserting and cutting. The body actions are: evading, turning, bending, diving, thrusting, bumping, squeezing, and leaning. The leg actions are: treading, ejecting, kicking, leaping, stamping, inserting and skimming. The foot actions are: advancing, retreating, circling, sticking-in, dashing and turning. The eye actions are: fixing, staring, following and gazing. In fine, Cha Boxing demands coordination of eyes, hands and postures and involves much jumping and turning. It demands to move right first when intending to move left and to retreat first when intending to advance. It comprises ten series of moves: Mother-Child Boxing, Waving-Hand Boxing, Kicking-Foot Boxing, Leveling Boxing, Northeast Boxing, Ambush Boxing, Plum Boxing, Chain Boxing, Dragon Tail Boxing and Interlocked Boxing. The first and second series have each an auxiliary series. In addition, there are series of moves with weapons, such as the sword, spear, hook and knife series of moves. There are also practising series of moves for building the foundation, such as Cannon Boxing, Sliding Boxing, Hong Boxing, Leg Boxing and Ten Kicks Boxing. A part of Cha Boxing series have been included in the specified Long Boxing series and have been used as martial arts teaching materials in the sports colleges in different parts of China.

Taiji Boxing was named after the term "tai ji" (supreme ultimate) from *Book of Changes*, believed to be composed by King Wen of the Zhou Dynasty. The term means that the universe was an entirety before it divided into heaven and earth. The Taiji Boxing prevailing in the recent one hundred years has been sourced from many forms of folk boxing, and has been improved on through several generations.

Taiji Boxing is characterized by the unification of mind, breath and motions (body), requiring concentration of mind and calmness of motions. "Mind works as a commander and body a soldier;" "When in motion all of the body moves. When at rest, all of the body rests." "Calmness is required for motion. " Simple force is not preferred. Force is like a wheel and waist is its axis. The motions are continuous as a circle. The breath is deep and controlled by the diaphragm. Be concentrated, gentle and natural. Be stable as a mountain when not moving, and be flowing as a river when moving. The moves are characterized by roundness, softness, slowness, stability and evenness. They are extended but very well coordinated, and all are an antithetical unity of Yin and Yang (negative and postive). These principles are the same for all schools of Taiji Boxing, though their types are different. There are mainly five types: Chen-Type, Yang-Type, Wuu-Type, Wu- Type, and Sun-Type.

Chen-Type Taiji Boxing was founded by a distinguished boxer Chen Wangting at the turn of the Ming Dynasty. According to *Chronicles of Wen County*, he was appointed the commander of the local garrison at the 14th year of the reign of Chongzhen of Emperor Si of Ming. After the Ming Dynasty was overthrown, he returned to his home village. Later, he formulated the Chen-Type Taiji Boxing and taught disciples and his scions.

Yang-Type Taiji Boxing was fostered by Yang Luchan, a native of Yongnian county in Hebei Province. He learned Chen-Type Taiji Boxing from Chen Changxing in Wen county of Henan Province. With the assistance of his son Yang Jianhou and his grandson Yang Chenpu, he remodelled the old Chen-Type Taiji Boxing, deleting the leaping, shaking feet and spurting moves. Later, Yang Jianhou remoulded it into the middle postures and Yang Chenpu, remodelled it into the large postures, which is the now popular Yang-Type Taiji Boxing.

Wuu-Type Taiji Boxing was founded by Wuu Yuxiang, also a native of Yongnian county in Hebei Province. He learned Chen-Type Taiji Boxing from his fellow countryman Yang Luchan. Then he learned from Chen Qingping the Zhaobao-Type Taiji Boxing. After revising it, he founded Wuu-Type Taiji Boxing.

Wu-Type Taiji Boxing sprang out in Beijing. When Yang Luchan taught boxing in Beijing after he founded the Yang-type, Wu Quanyou, a Manchu soldier stationed in Beijing, learned from Yang Luchan the boxing skills. Then he learned from Yang Banhou again, the son of the Yang-type founder, and became a famous master of boxing himself. Finally he initiated Wu-Type Taiji Boxing.

Sun-Type Taiji Boxing was founded by Sun Lutang. Born in Wan county of Hebei Province, Sun learned Form Boxing first from Li Kuihuan and then from Guo Yunshen, the teacher of Li. Then he learned

Eight Trigram Boxing from Cheng Tinghua. He became very skilled in boxing after many years of learning. Finally he learned from Hao Weizhen Taiji Boxing. Blending the quintessence of Eight-Trigram Boxing, Form Boxing and Taiji Boxing, he established Sun-Type Taiji Boxing.

Among the legacies of Chinese martial arts Emei School, Shaolin School and Wudang School are of tripartite importance. As commented by Monk Zhang Ran at the beginning of the Qing Dynasty, "Emei School is as Five blossoms in a tree held by eight leaves; The bright moon above Mount Emei shines in the martial-arts field. " (Zhan Ran: *Emei Boxing Shop*) The Emei School combines the Daoist dynamic martial arts and the Buddhist static martial arts. The dynamic exercises comprise twelve exercises: "Heaven, Earth, Zigzag, Mind, Dragon, Crane, Wind, Cloud, Great, Minor, Secluded, and Profound exercises." The static exercises comprise six exercises: "Tiger-Pace, Heavy-Thump, Shrink, Suspend, the Fingering and Nirvana exercises",

A Pair of Bronze Hammers

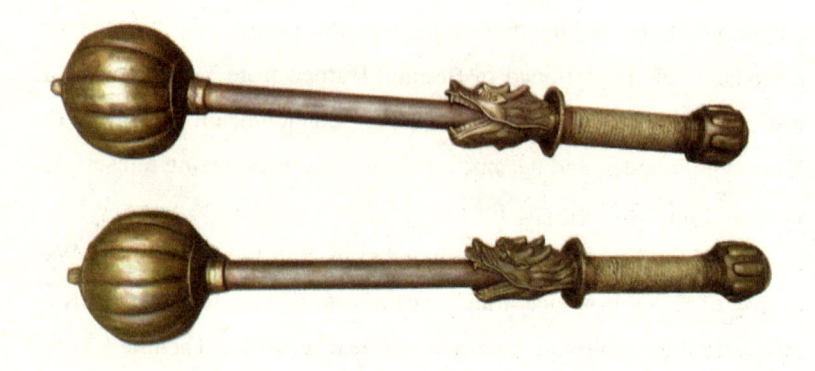

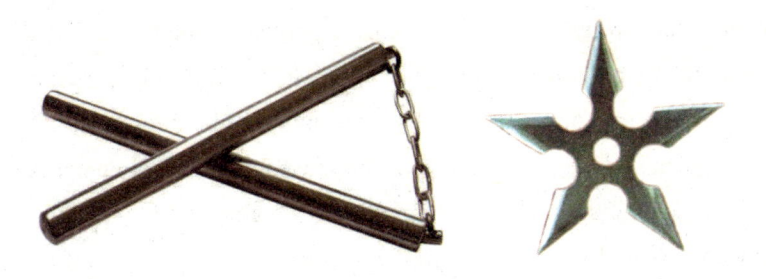

A Nunchakus staff   A Dart in the Shape of Pentagram

of which the 36-postures Fingering Exercises were most powerful, used in massage and in subduing opponents. Emei School stresses the moves with "five peaks" (head, shoulder, elbow, buttocks and knee) and "six elbows" (upper elbow, lower elbow, left elbow, right elbow, circular elbow and reverse elbow). In attack and defence, it stresses nimbleness of hands and feet, chiefly in "jumping, shifting, dodging, somersaulting, drifting, sinking, swallowing and vomiting".

Exercises with weapons are a very important part of Chinese martial arts. The weapons employed in the exercises include broadsword, sword, spear, cudgel, double-broadswords, double - swords, double-spears, double-hooks, nine-sectionwhip, rope hammer, rope dart, etc. The most popular weapons are broad sword, sword, spear and cudgel. The chief moves with broadsword are: head-harassing, splitting, cutting, stirring, and trailing, aided by auxiliary moves of the other hand, pacing and jumping, and characterized by boldness and power. The moves with sword are: touching, bursting, stabbing, stirring, splitting and trailing, aided by pointing with the other hand and pacing, and are characterized by swiftness, briskness, fierceness, suppleness, and gracefulness. The moves with spear comprise basically intercepting, pricking, and brandishing; characterized by combination of fierceness, suppleness, and changefulness. The moves with cudgel comprise chiefly swinging, splitting, stabbing, stirring, hoeing and brandishing, characterized by fierceness, swiftness and power.

There are "eighteen kinds of weapons" in Chinese martial arts, though they are interpreted differently. Deleting the repetitions of the different interpretations, they are projectiles, including bow, crossbow, arrow, rocket, etc. ; long weapons, including dagger-axe, spear, lance, cudgel, pestle, pole, stick, club, axe, scratcher, halberd, broadsword, grasper, rake, knocker and spade; short weapons, including sword, short handle broadsword, whip, mace, hook, sickle, hammer, crutch and hoop; and soft weapons, including chain, rope, dart and lasso. Martial arts without weapons are generally called barehanded martial arts. All the above gives a sketch of the ancient Chinese martial arts.

❷ Chinese Martial Arts, an Aspect of Chinese Cultrue

Chinese martial arts are an organic component of the Chinese culture. They reflect the entire Chinese cultural characteristics from one aspect.

Chinese martial arts have a long history, converging Chinese philosophy, medicine, military strategy, techniques, education, aesthetics, etc. , and mirroring the character and sagacity of the Chinese people. The Chinese martial arts pay great attention to mental activities in

Performing Qigong

fighting. They stress that mind should guide breath, breath should guide the motions of the body, that hands, eyes and pacing, spirit, breath and force, ferociousness and agility, the external and the internal, all should be coordinated, and that motions should be changeful and rhythmic. In addition, they stress winning through cunning and taking advantage of the opponent's momentums, keeping the foothold firm, the waist nimble and the head safe. The martial arts practisers do not mind to retreat a step first so as to be justified, advantageous and well controlled. The martial arts practisers hit surely, accurately and forcefully, but put sureness in the first place.

The shaping of the Chinese martial arts results from three sources: philosophy and science, technical development and tutoring. The Chinese classic philosophy is the principle of the Chinese martial arts. The classic military stratagems are their contesting principles. The traditional medicine is their exercising principle. The technical development of the Chinese martial arts corresponds with the development of the classic culture and technique, particularly with the development of combating methods, artistic interests and hygiene. They underwent three phases. The first phase was the phase of bravery, based on strength and bravery; The second phase was the phase of martial skills, based on tactics and skills; The third phase is the phase of martial arts exercises based on standardization and stylization.

The course of the first phase involves blending ancient health preserving technique with fighting and grappling technique.

The course of the second phase involves typifying some fighting and grappling moves, and combining them with the art of dancing and acrobatics.

The course of the third phase involves combining body training with mind training, and adopting a set of "personality cultivating" technique to "coordinate body and mind".

The top concern of the Chinese martial arts is to settle the relationship between body and the mind. They stress the "external exercises for bones and muscles and internal exercises for breath". All the schools of martial arts stress "presence of mind, breath and strength" , so as to equilibrate Yin & Yang, regulate breath and blood, smoothen channels and collaterals, and build up body and strength. They settle the relationship between "form and content" of martial arts by settling the relationship between mind and body and the relationship between oneself and his opponent. They all stress "changing according to different opponents", and "getting opportunities through defending." The functions of the martial arts in fighting are: defending oneself against the opponent, checking the attacks and winning the fight. On the level of philosophy, the martial arts stress "unification of man and nature", i. e., the unification of existence and nonexistence, acting and stopping, Yin and Yang, mind and things, the subjective and objective, and the objective law and the subjective dynamism. On the social level, the martial arts stress cultivation of mind and personality, awareness of the natural law and complacency. Thus they break all prejudices with regard to winning and losing and to successes and failures, and take a calm, "game" attitude. In fighting, the exercisers of the martial arts play calmly as in a game, with a free and initiative attitude. Therefore, the Chinese martial arts are not simply a sport event or a fighting technique, but thinking, a style, a life attitude and a personality cultivation. In a contest with an opponent the Chinese martial arts exercisers not only take a great care about the moves, and exertion of force, but also take a great care about his own temperament and mind, with a martial arts spirit transcending mere technique.

③ Breathing Exercise of Chinese Martial Arts

Breathing exercise (Qigong) is practised to strengthen physique and exploit human body potential energy in Chinese martial arts. In a broad sense, it is not just a method, but is a theory related to human body potentials. In the present day, Qigong can be classified into the following types:

Soul-Particle Type (spontaneous type) is said to have been practised by real ancient witches and wizards who believed that inside the human body exists the "soul particle", a necessary matter of the human soul and a carrier of human sub-consciousness. The key to exercising this is to let one's soul particle control oneself and to let one's subsciouness make spontaneous moves, so that the human potential energy can be strengthened through the exercises. The exercises were chiefly used to cure diseases and injuries of oneself and others. Its representative exercise is the Soul-Particle-Motion Technique.

The Internal Elixir Type was originally founded by Daoists as a part of alchemy. But also some Confucian scholars took part in it on the basis of the ideas in *Book of Changes*. So, this type was a mixed product of Daoists and Confucian scholars, which was greatly improved. Exponents of this type believe that practising this type of exercises will result in longevity, as if one has taken the elixir. Because of this belief and the pursuit of people for longevity, the Internal Elixir Type has become the mainstream of breathing exercises. It has formed a complete, complicated system aiming at the "great way" or longevity, not at any magic power.

The Martial-Arts Type does not have a defined origin. It cultivates the internal energy in human body. By stimulating this internal energy temporarily in some way, one can beat the opponent. Examples of this type are the light moving exercise, and the hard breathing exercise.

The Tibet, an Secret Type originated from Tibet, entirely for exploiting the human potential energy. It has developed a complete theoretical system with varied processes ranging from the ordinary processes to the high yoga processes. Its features are: murmuring the incantations, holding the seal and conceiving the wonder. But according to a general rule, the exerciser can only practise it after he is accepted to be a disciple of a suitable master. Such opportunities are so rare that they depend on predestination.

Other types include Indian Yoga and Western hypnotism.

What is meant by Qi (breath) is energy. That is to gather energy through mobilization of it by mind. Breathing Exercise (Qigong) is for gathering the energy. Energy consumption is required for metabolism, for working of the viscera and for manual and mental labor. "Man lives on a breath. " When breathing is suspended, energy is exhausted and life expires.

The Daoists have devised over a hundred methods for breathing exercises for achieving mental calmness and conserving energy, including the static, dynamic, and dynamic-static methods. The static methods are the main ones. There are about five chief methods for static breathing exercise—the Mind Cultivation, the Breath Cultivation, the Mind Preservation, the Apertures Conservation, and the Internal Elixir methods.